STORMY WEATHER

◆

THE RADICAL IMAGINATION SERIES
Edited by Henry A. Giroux and Stanley Aronowitz

Now Available

Beyond the Spectacle of Terrorism: Global Uncertainty and the Challenge of the New Media
    by Henry A. Giroux

Global Modernity
    by Arif Dirlik

Stormy Weather: Katrina and the Politics of Disposability
    by Henry A. Giroux

Forthcoming

Left Turn: Forging a New Political Future
    by Stanley Aronowitz

Afromodernity: How Europe Is Evolving toward Africa
    by Jean Comaroff and John L. Comaroff

STORMY WEATHER
Katrina and the
Politics of Disposability

HENRY A. GIROUX

Paradigm Publishers
Boulder • London

Copyright © 2006 by Paradigm Publishers

Published in the United States by Paradigm Publishers, 3360 Mitchell Lane Suite E, Boulder, Colorado 80301 USA.

Paradigm Publishers is the trade name of Birkenkamp & Company, LLC, Dean Birkenkamp, President and Publisher.

Library of Congress Cataloging-in-Publication Data

Giroux, Henry A.
   Stormy weather : Katrina and the politics of disposability / by Henry A. Giroux.
      p. cm.
   ISBN-13: 978-1-59451-328-2 (hc)
   ISBN-10: 1-59451-328-7 (hc)
   ISBN-13: 978-1-59451-329-9 (pb)
   ISBN-10: 1-59451-329-5 (pb)
   1. Marginality, Social—United States.   2. People with social disabilities—Government policy—United States.   3. Racism—United States.   4. Neoliberalism—United States.   5. Hurricane Katrina, 2005—Social aspects.   6. United States—Politics and government—1989–   7. United States—Race relations.   I. Title.
   HN90.M26G57 2006
   305.5'60976090511—dc22
                                                                    2006012177

Printed and bound in the United States of America on acid-free paper that meets the standards of the American National Standard for Permanence of Paper for Printed Library Materials.

Designed and Typeset by Straight Creek Bookmakers.

10   09   08   07   06   1   2   3   4   5

For Susan, my muse and heartbeat.

Contents

◇

Acknowledgments

I want to thank Susan Searls Giroux and Roger Simon for providing me with a number of critical insights and suggestions that otherwise would not have been in this book. While I am solely responsible for the contents, their critical input was invaluable in helping me think through the various ideas I take up in this piece. I also want to thank Arif Dirlik, Zygmunt Bauman, David Clark, John Comaroff, Ken Saltman, Max Haiven, and Scott Stoneman for their critical input. I am deeply indebted to my graduate assistant, Grace Pollock, for greatly improving this manuscript by bringing to bear her creative and critical editorial skills. And my administrative assistant, Maya Stamenkovic, again provided invaluable support.

◇

1

Katrina and the Biopolitics of Disposability

*When it thunders and lightnin' and when the
    wind begins to blow
When it thunders and lightnin' and the wind
    begins to blow
There's thousands of people ain't got no place
    to go*
                                    —*Bessie Smith*

Emmett Till's body arrived home in Chicago in September 1955. White racists in Mississippi had tortured, mutilated, and killed the young 14–year-old African-American boy for whistling at a white woman. Determined to make visible the horribly mangled face and twisted body of the child as an expression of racial hatred and killing, Mamie Till, the boy's mother, insisted that the coffin, interred at the A. A. Ranier Funeral Parlor on the South Side of Chicago, be left open for four long days. While mainstream news organizations ignored the horrifying image, *Jet* magazine published an unedited photo of Till's face taken while he lay in his coffin. Shaila Dewan points out that "[m]utilated is the word most often used to describe the face of Emmett Till after his body was hauled out of the Tallahatchie river in Mississippi. Inhuman is more like it: melted, bloated, missing an eye, swollen so large that its patch of wiry hair looks like that of a balding old man, not a handsome, brazen 14–year-old boy."[1] The *Jet* photos not only made visible the violent effects of the racial state; they also fueled massive public anger, especially among blacks, and helped to launch the Civil Rights Movement.

From the beginning of the Civil Rights Movement to the war in Vietnam, images of human suffering and violence provided the grounds for a charged political indignation and collective sense of moral outrage inflamed by the horrors of poverty, militarism, war, and racism—eventually mobilizing widespread opposition to these anti-democratic forces. Of course, the seeds of a vast conservative counterrevolution were already well under way as images of a previous era—"whites only" signs, segregated schools, segregated housing, and nonviolent resistance—gave way to a troubling iconography of cities aflame, mass rioting, and armed black youth who came to embody the very precepts of lawlessness, disorder, and criminality. Building on the reactionary rhetorics of Barry Goldwater and Richard Nixon, Ronald Reagan took office in 1980 with a trickle-down theory that would transform corporate America and a corresponding visual economy. The twin images of the young black male "gangsta" and his counterpart, the "welfare queen," became the primary vehicles for selling the American public on the need to dismantle the welfare state, ushering in an era of unprecedented deregulation, downsizing, privatization, and regressive taxation. The propaganda campaign was so successful that George H. W. Bush could launch his 1988 presidential bid with the image of Willie Horton, an African-American male convicted of rape and granted early release, and succeed in trouncing his opponent with little public outcry over the overtly racist nature of the campaign. By the beginning of the 1990s, global media consolidation, coupled with the outbreak of a new war that encouraged hyper-patriotism and a rigid nationalism, resulted in a tightly controlled visual landscape—managed both by the Pentagon and by corporate-owned networks—that delivered a paucity of images representative of the widespread systemic violence.[2] Selectively informed and cynically inclined, American civic life became more sanitized, controlled, and regulated.

Since the 1990s there has been a drying up of images that make the violence of war, poverty, and racism visible in the United States. The domestic war of images largely won, the administration of George H. W. Bush retooled for the war abroad. Learning a lesson from the Vietnam War, it tried to control both the style of the news and the release of visual images that accompanied the reporting of the Gulf War in 1991. Unpleasant images of the war were either censored or white-washed. Under the auspices of the Defense Department and a corporate media all too willing to do the government's bidding in exchange for further deregulation by the FCC, the concept of war was aestheticized. Soldiers framed against the backdrop of a blazing sunset replaced mangled bodies and bloodied wounds. Air strikes were morphed into video games, and images of battle were craftily packaged by the advertising gurus of the government-friendly public relations firm Hill and Knowlton. Increasingly, the public's right to know was replaced with an official policy of misrepresentation, distortion, and secrecy. The National Security Archive acknowledges that "[t]he practice of permitting media coverage of fallen soldiers' return to the United States was curtailed in 1991, during the Gulf War."[3]

Within a decade, the American visual landscape had once again been utterly transformed. The multiracial make-up of the George W. Bush administration succeeded in selling the lie of a race-transcendent, color-blind, and meritocratic nation, effectively silencing critical inquiry and debate over widening racial inequality and injustice in mainstream political coverage. Why meet with the NAACP, the president once quipped, when he sits in daily meetings with Colin Powell and Condoleezza Rice? With domestic race relations a dead issue, with the single exception of affirmative action, which he condemns, President Bush and his minions focused their energies on managing the second Gulf War. The anti-democratic confluence of censorship and secrecy has become one of the Bush administration's defining and vigorously defended principles. Once again, the Pentagon resurrected the practice of prohibiting photographs of the flag-draped caskets of the dead returning from war. With the advent of the Internet, representations of the bodies of mangled civilians, children, and others who are not soldiers can be found on *Al Jazeera* and other alternative media sites, especially in the Middle East and Europe, but are rarely seen in the mainstream media in the United States. This visual absence is further reinforced by the government's Orwellian language of collateral damage, often disappearing into a state- and media-sponsored fog of secrecy and censorship. Instead of providing images of the real consequences of war, the Bush administration and the dominant media present images of the Gulf War that offer viewers a visual celebration of high-tech weaponry and earthy down-home grit on the part of American soldiers. President George W. Bush's initial bombardment of Baghdad was introduced to the public through the metaphor of "shock and awe," one that prioritized slick advertising over human suffering and offered up representations of the attack modeled after a giant Fourth of July fireworks display. "Embedded" reporters were often transformed into daring postmodern cowboys riding in armored tanks, fitted with the latest high-tech weapons and photographed against pristine images of the desert, producing war images in which immediacy replaced context. Modeled on the familiar Reality TV show, media representations of the war celebrated the ethos of militarism, obedience, discipline, and technological mastery. Theatricality replaced substance, and aesthetics triumphed over politics.[4] Representations of war and violence were increasingly staged as a global spectacle, diminishing the critical functions of sound, image, and language along with the critical capacities of viewers. But there was more at work here than the residual return of a kind of fascist aesthetics. There was also the struggle over representations of agency, masculinity, patriotism, and national values.

In many ways, the second Iraq war, as Bill Moyers pointed out, has become a "war of images."[5] When Ted Koppel, host of the television show *Nightline,* announced that he was going to read the names and show pictures of the U.S. soldiers who had died in Iraq (721 as of that day), Sinclair Broadcasting, owner of no fewer than sixty-two television stations, blacked out the faces and names when the program aired on its ABC affiliate stations. According to the Sinclair Broadcast Group, Koppel's actions were deemed subversive and unpatriotic and "would undermine public opinion."[6] Even when the war's positive-image brigade hit a rough patch with the scandal at Abu Ghraib, the media barely blinked. The editor of the *New York Post* announced after the *60 Minutes II* story "shocked the world with photos of U.S. military personnel abusing and torturing Iraqis" held in Abu Ghraib prison that "he would not run the photos because 'a handful of U.S. soldiers' shouldn't be allowed to 'reflect poorly' on the 140,000 who do their job well.'"[7] Political-image management took a major hit with the publication of the Abu Ghraib prison photos. Government officials played down the incident, claiming it involved only a handful of soldiers and refusing to release additional images they had confiscated. With now-characteristic gall, a few supporters of the Bush administration, such as Republican Oklahoma Senator James Inhofe, claimed that the real problem was not the acts of abuse and torture at Abu Ghraib but the liberal media's decision to release such images to the public. Of course, Seymour Hersh and a number of other journalists later proved that the horrendous abuses and tortures at Abu Ghraib were neither limited to one prison nor merely the result of a few "bad apples."[8] As is now commonly known, such practices were justified at the highest levels of government. Tragically, as disturbing as these pictures were, they were never fully represented and understood "as part of the dynamic of military culture and the experience of war" against populations of color.[9] This particular breach of Pentagon control seems to have exhausted its capacity for mobilizing either collective reflection or outrage and social action.

In a few instances over the last two decades, individual citizens used new media technologies to challenge this type of collective censorship and made public some of the deeply disturbing and defining contradictions shaping American life. For instance, a videotape made in 1992 of the vicious beating of an African-American man, Rodney King, by four Los Angeles police officers shattered the conservative discourse about color-blindness, the end of racism, and the media's utter complicity with the residual force of the racial state.[10] More recently, as new media technologies such as the Internet, digital photography, and electronically mediated forms of communication emerge and convey information at a higher velocity than ever before, it has become more difficult to prevent disturbing images and photographs from reaching the American public. As David Simpson points out, "It is not news that all images are subject to both direct and self-imposed political control. Private Jessica Lynch, for example, had the independence of mind to resent the falsifications of her captivity narrative for propaganda purposes and the courage to say so."[11] Unfortunately, she was quietly dropped from any major media attention when she exposed the government's fabricated lie about her capture in Iraq.

Hurricane Katrina may have reversed the self-imposed silence of the media and public numbness in the face of terrible suffering. Fifty years after the body of Emmett Till was plucked out of the mud-filled waters of the Tallahatchie River, another set of troubling visual representations has emerged that both shocked and shamed the nation. In the aftermath of Hurricane Katrina, grotesque images of bloated corpses floating in the rotting waters that flooded the streets of New Orleans circulated throughout the mainstream media. What first appeared to be a natural catastrophe soon degenerated into a social debacle as further images revealed, days after Katrina had passed over the Gulf Coast, hundreds of thousands of poor people—mostly blacks, some Latinos, many elderly, and a few white people—packed into the New Orleans Superdome and the city's convention center, stranded on rooftops, or isolated on patches of dry highway without any food, water, or any place to wash, urinate, or find relief from the scorching sun.[12] Weeks passed as the flood water gradually receded and the military gained control of the city, and more images of dead bodies surfaced in the national and global media. TV cameras rolled as bodies emerged on dry patches of land where people stood by indifferently eating their lunch or occasionally snapping a photograph. The world watched in disbelief as bloated decomposing bodies left on the street—or, in some cases, on the porches of once-flooded homes—were broadcast on CNN. Most of the bodies found in the flood water "were 50 or older, people who tried to wait the hurricane out."[13] A body that had been found on a dry stretch of Union Street in the downtown district of New Orleans remained on the street for four days, "locked in rigor mortis and flanked by traffic cones. [It quickly] became a downtown landmark—as in, turn left at the corpse—before someone" finally picked it up.[14] Responding to this human indignity, Dan Barry, a writer for the *New York Times,* observed: "That a corpse lies on Union Street may not shock.... What is remarkable is that on a downtown street in a major American city, a corpse can decompose for days, like a carrion, and that is acceptable."[15] Alcede Jackson's 72–year-old black body was left on the porch of his house for two weeks. Various media soon reported that over 154 bodies had been found in hospitals and nursing homes. The *New York Times* wrote that "the collapse of one of society's most basic covenants—to care for the helpless—suggests that the elderly and critically ill plummeted to the bottom of priority lists as calamity engulfed New Orleans."[16] Dead people, mostly poor African-Americans, left uncollected in the streets, on porches, and in hospitals, nursing homes, electric wheelchairs, and collapsed houses, prompted some people to claim that America had become like a "Third World country" while others argued that New Orleans resembled a "Third World Refugee Camp."[17] There were now, irrefutably, two Gulf crises. The Federal Emergency Management Agency tried to do damage control by forbidding journalists to "accompany rescue boats as they went out to search for storm victims." As a bureau spokeswoman told Reuters News Agency, "We have requested that no photographs of the deceased be made by the media."[18] But questions about responsibility and answerability would not go away. Even the dominant media for a short time rose to the occasion of posing tough questions about accountability to those in power in light of such egregious acts of incompetence and indifference.

The images of dead bodies kept reappearing in New Orleans, refusing to go away. For many, the bodies of the poor, black, brown, elderly, and sick came to signify what the battered body of Emmett Till once unavoidably revealed, and America was forced to confront these disturbing images and the damning questions behind the images. The Hurricane Katrina disaster, like the Emmett Till affair, revealed a vulnerable and destitute segment of the nation's citizenry that conservatives not only refused to see but had spent the better part of two decades demonizing. But like the incessant beating of Poe's tell-tale heart, cadavers have a way of insinuating themselves on consciousness, demanding answers to questions that aren't often asked. The body of Emmett Till symbolized an overt white supremacy and state terrorism organized against the threat that black men (apparently of all sizes and ages) posed against white women. But the black bodies of the dead and walking wounded in New Orleans in 2005 revealed a different image of the racial state, a different modality of state terrorism marked less by an overt form of white racism than by a highly mediated displacement of race as a central concept for understanding both Katrina and its place in the broader history of U.S. racism.[19] That is, while Till's body insisted upon a public recognition of the violence of white supremacy, the decaying black bodies floating in the waters of the Gulf Coast represented a return of race against the media and public insistence that this disaster was more about class than race, more about the shameful and growing presence of poverty, "the abject failure to provide aid to the most vulnerable."[20] Till's body allowed the racism that destroyed it to be made visible, to speak to the systemic character of American racial injustice. The bodies of the Katrina victims could not speak with the same directness to the state of American racist violence, but they did reveal and shatter the conservative fiction of living in a color-blind society.

The bodies that repeatedly appeared all over New Orleans days and weeks after it was struck by Hurricane Katrina laid bare the racial and class fault lines that mark an increasingly damaged and withering democracy and reveal the emergence of a new kind of politics—one in which entire populations are now considered disposable, an unnecessary burden on state coffers, and consigned to fend for themselves. The deeply existential and material questions regarding who is going to die and who is going to live in this society are now centrally determined by race and class.[21] Katrina lays bare what many people in the United States do not want to see: large numbers of poor black and brown people struggling to make ends meet, benefiting very little from a social system that makes it difficult to obtain health insurance, child care, social assistance, cars, savings, and minimum-wage jobs if lucky, and instead offers to black and brown youth inadequate schools, poor public services, and no future, except a possible stint in the

penitentiary. As Janet Pelz rightly insists, "These are
the people the Republicans have been teaching us to
disdain, if not hate, since President Reagan decried
the moral laxness of the Welfare mom."[22] While Pelz's
comments provide a crucial context for much of the
death and devastation of Katrina, I think to more fully
understand this calamity it is important to grasp how
the confluence of race and poverty has become part
of a new and more insidious set of forces based on a
revised set of biopolitical commitments, which have
largely given up on the sanctity of human life for those
populations rendered "at risk" by global neoliberal
economies and, instead, have embraced an emergent
security state founded on cultural homogeneity.

In what follows, I want to offer a reading of the Hurricane Katrina tragedy that contradicts conventional
accounts of the disaster, even those critical of the
Bush administration. The events surrounding Katrina
are about more than incompetence, lack of compassion, and ignorance; they are the consequence of a
systemic, violent form of social engineering in which
those populations in the United States marginalized
by race and class are now considered disposable—that
is, simply collateral damage in the construction of a
neoliberal order.

Rethinking Biopolitics

The pictures and news reports are unbelievable—
people waiting, starving and dehydrated ... and
a famous football stadium that became a death
trap. The elderly slumped on baggage carousels at
the airport—some dead, some dying. The contrast
between the enormous wealth of our country,
with its massive stadiums and transportation

infrastructure, and the desperate human suffering, the collapse of civilization and humanity in
New Orleans, makes a shocking picture.[23]

Within the last few decades, matters of state sovereignty in the new world order have been retheorized
so as to provide a range of theoretical insights about
the relationship between power and politics, the political nature of social and cultural life, and the merging
of life and politics as a new form of biopolitics. While
the notion of biopolitics differs significantly among its
most prominent theorists, including Michel Foucault,
Giorgio Agamben, and Michael Hardt and Antonio Negri,[24] what these theorists share is an attempt to think
through the convergence of life and politics, locating
matters of "life and death within our ways of thinking
about and imagining politics."[25] Central here is the
task of reformulating the meaning of politics and how
it functions within the contemporary moment to regulate matters of life and death, and, in turn, how such
issues are intimately related to both the articulation
of community and the social, and the regulation, care,
and development of human life. Within this discourse,
politics is no longer understood exclusively through
a disciplinary technology centered on the individual
body—a body to be measured, surveilled, managed,
included in forecasts, surveys, and statistical projec-
tions. Under the new biopolitical regimes, the body is
understood primarily as an object of power, but it is a
body that is social and multiple, scientific and ideological. Biopolitics points to new relations of power that
are more capacious, concerned not only with the body
as an object of disciplinary techniques that render it
"both useful and docile" but with a body that needs to
be "regularized," subject to those immaterial means
of production that produce ways of life that enlarge

the targets of control and regulation.[26] This shift in the workings of both sovereignty and power and the emergence of a new form of biopower and biopolitics are made clear by Foucault. He writes:

> Beneath that great absolute power, beneath the dramatic and somber absolute power that was the power of sovereignty, and which consisted in the power to take life, we now have the emergence, with this technology of biopower, of this technology of power over "the" population as such, over men insofar as they are living beings. It is continuous, scientific, and it is the power to make live. Sovereignty took life and let live. And now we have the emergence of power that I would call the power of regularization, and it, in contrast, consists in making live and *letting die.*[27] (emphasis added)

For Foucault, biopolitics implies that sovereignty has moved away from disciplinary technologies in which power is defined by the right to take life and impose death toward a form of biopower that replaces the power to dispense fear and death "with that of a power to foster life—or disallow it to the point of death.... [Biopower] is no longer a matter of bringing death into play in the field of sovereignty, but of distributing the living in the domain of value and utility. Its task is to take charge of life that needs a continuous regulatory and corrective mechanism."[28] As Foucault insists, the logic of biopower is dialectical, productive, and positive: "It exerts a positive influence on life, endeavours to administer, optimize, and multiply it."[29] Yet, while Foucault understands the singular importance of biopolitics to foster life as its object and objective, making, producing and expanding the possibility of

what it means to live as its central and primary function, he also argues that biopolitics does not remove
itself from "introducing a break into the domain of life
that is under power's control: the break between what
must live and what must die."[30] Foucault believes that
the death-function in the economy of biopolitics is
justified primarily through a form of racism in which
biopower "is bound up with the workings of a State
that is obliged to use race, the elimination of races
and the purification of the race, to exercise its sovereign power."[31]

Michael Hardt and Antonio Negri have both modi-
fied and extended Foucault's notion of biopower. Their
somewhat overgeneralized, yet insightful, version of
the concept differs from Foucault's more grounded historical and genealogical analyses of its workings within
different contexts and social formations. Biopower
for Hardt and Negri highlights a mode of biopolitics
in which immaterial labor such as ideas, knowledge,
images, cooperation, affective relations, and forms of
communication extend beyond the boundaries of the
economic to produce not just material goods as "the
means of social life but social life itself. Immaterial
production is biopolitical."[32] In this instance, power
is extended to the educational force of the culture
and to the various technologies, mechanisms, and
social practices through which it reproduces various
forms of social life. What is crucial to grasp in this
rather generalized notion of biopolitics is that power
remains a productive force, provides the grounds for
both resistance and domination, and registers culture,
society, and politics as a terrain of multiple and diverse struggles waged by numerous groups in a wide
range of sites. More specifically, biopower for Hardt
and Negri registers a global world in which production
is not merely economic but social—"the production

of communications, relationships, and forms of life" that allows the multitude "to manage to communicate and act in common while remaining internally differ- ent," yet sharing a common currency in the desire for democracy.[33] And it is precisely within this new form of biopolitics that Hardt and Negri believe new and diverse social subjects sharing a common project of resistance and democracy can emerge on a global scale.

For my purposes, the importance of both Foucault's and Hardt and Negri's works on biopolitics, in spite of their distinct theoretical differences, is that they move matters of culture, especially those aimed at "the production of information, communication, [and] social relations[,] ... to the center of politics itself."[34] Within these approaches, power expands its reach as a political force beyond the traditional range and boundaries of the state and the registers of officially sanctioned modes of domination. As Paul Rabinow and Nikolas Rose observe, biopolitics, especially in Foucault's account,

> serves to bring into view a field comprised of more or less rationalised attempts to intervene upon the vital characteristics of human existence—hu- man beings, individually and collectively, as living creatures who are born, mature, inhabit a body that can be trained and augmented, and then sicken and die as collectivities or populations composed of such living beings.[35]

In both Foucault and Hardt and Negri, modernity represents a transition in which traditional forms of sovereign power and authority give way to more disciplinary modes of confinement and control. In postmodernity, disciplinary power is not replaced but complicated by the emergence in the twentieth century of new modes of biopower. Subjects are now inscribed in orders of power and knowledge in which various technologies—extending from surveillance and population control to genetic manipulation—work not only on the individual body but also through "modes of subjectification through which individuals work on themselves."[36] Within this notion of biopolitics, life and politics merge, and the struggle over life and death is increasingly played out in a variety of arenas and spheres, domestically and globally.[37]

Both Foucault and Hardt and Negri understand biopolitics largely through its productive capacity. For Foucault, biopower no longer resembles the classical sovereign notion of control "exercised mainly as a means of deduction—the seizing of things, time, bodies, and ultimately the seizing of life itself."[38] Instead, biopower now registers the multiple ways in which power is organized through precise controls and comprehensive regulations to exercise a positive influence on the life of the species. For Hardt and Negri, the biopolitical signals "a form of power that regulates social life from its interior,"[39] mediated through the world of ideas, knowledge, new modes of communication, and a proliferating multitude of diverse social relations. Biopolitics now touches all aspects of social life and is the primary political and pedagogical force through which the creation and reproduction of new subjectivities take place. According to Hardt and Negri, "Who we are, how we view the world, how we interact with each other are all created through this social, biopolitical production."[40]

While biopolitics in Foucault and Hardt and Negri addresses the relations between politics and death, biopolitics in their views is less concerned with the primacy of death than with the production of life both as an individual and a social category. For Giorgio Agamben, such a relationship is not only rejected as historically inaccurate but also is absolutely untrue in the current historical conjuncture.[41] Biopower in Agamben's formulation is the administration of what he calls "bare life," and its ultimate incarnation is the Holocaust with its ominous specter of the concentration camp. In this formulation, the Nazi death camps become the primary exemplar of control, the new space of contemporary politics in which individuals are no longer viewed as citizens but are now seen as inmates, stripped of everything, including their right to live. The uniting of power and bare life, the reduction of the individual to *homo sacer*—the sacred man who under certain states of exception "may be killed and yet not sacrificed"—no longer represents the far end of political life.[42] That is, in this updated version of the ancient category of *homo sacer* is the human who stands beyond the confines of both human and divine law—"a human who can be killed without fear of punishment but cannot be used in religious sacrifice."[43] According to Agamben, as modern states increasingly suspend their democratic structures, laws, and principles, the very nature of governance changes as "the rule of law is routinely displaced by the state of exception, or emergency, and people are increasingly subject to extra-judicial state violence."[44] The life unfit for life, unworthy of being lived, as the central category of *homo sacer,* is no longer marginal to sovereign power but is now central to its form of governance. State violence and totalitarian power, which, in the past, either were generally short-lived or existed on the fringe of politics and history, have now become the rule, rather than the exception, as life is more ruthlessly regulated and placed in the hands of military and state power. For Agamben, the coupling of the state of exception with the metaphor of bare life points to a notion of biopolitics that "registers the effects not so much of a new kind of power as the heightened impact of a force internal to the sovereign relation from the beginning."[45] Similarly, as Catherine Mills points out, in the current historical moment "all subjects are at least potentially if not actually abandoned by the law and exposed to violence as a constitutive condition of political existence."[46] Nicholas Mirzoeff has observed that all over the world there is a growing resentment of immigrants and refugees, matched by the emergence of detain-and-deport strategies coupled with the rise of the camp as the key institution and social model of the new millennium. The "empire of camps," according to Mirzoeff, has become the "exemplary institution of a system of global capitalism that supports the West in its high-consumption, low-price consumer lifestyle."[47] Bauman calls such camps "garrisons of extraterritoriality" and argues that they have become "the dumping grounds for the indisposed of and as yet unrecycled waste of the global frontier-land."[48] The regime of the camp has increasingly become a key index of modernity and the new world order. The connection among disposability, violence, and death has become common under modernity in those countries where the order of power has become necropolitical. For example, Rosa Linda Fregoso analyzes feminicide as a local expression of global violence against women in the region of the U.S./Mexico border where over one thousand women have either been murdered or disappeared, constituting what amounts to a "politics of gender extermination."[49] The politics of disposability and necropolitics not only generate widespread violence and ever-expanding "garrisons of extraterritoriality" but also have taken on a powerful new significance as a foundation for political sovereignty. Biopolitical commitments to "let die" by abandoning citizens appear increasingly credible in light of the growing authoritarianism in the United States under the Bush administration.[50]

Given the Bush administration's use of illegal wiretaps, the holding of "detainees" illegally and indefinitely in prisons such as Guantanamo, the disappearance, kidnapping, and torture of alleged terrorists, and the ongoing suspension of civil liberties in the United States, Agamben's theory of biopolitics rightly alerts us to the dangers of a government in which the state of emergency becomes the fundamental structure of control over populations. One of the more theoretically instructive questions that arises from Agamben's notion of biopolitics has been deftly posed by Achille Mbembe: "What is the relationship between politics and death in those systems that can function only in a state of emergency?"[51] While Agamben's claim that the concentration camp (as opposed to Foucault's panopticon) is now the model for constitutional states captures the contrariness of biopolitical commitments that have less to do with preserving life than with reproducing violence and death, its totalitarian logic is too narrow and, in the end, fails to recognize that the threat of violence, bare life, and death is not the only form of biopower in contemporary life. Rabinow and Rose reveal the limitations inherent in Agamben's formulation:

> The power to command under threat of death is exercised by States and their surrogates in multiple instances, in micro forms and in geopolitical relations. But this is not to say that this form of power—commands backed up by the ultimate threat of death—is the guaranteed or underpinning principle of *all forms of biopower*

in contemporary liberal societies. Reciprocally, it is obfuscating to use this single diagram to analyze every contemporary instance of thanato-politics—from Rwanda to the Lord's Resistance Army in Uganda, SARS or the epidemic of AIDS deaths across Africa. To analogise all other in-stances large and small where life or the body or health is at stake to this one exemplar is to do a profound and politically dangerous disservice to critical thought—for the essence of that thought must be its capacity to make distinctions that can facilitate judgement and action.[52] (emphasis added)

Agamben is surely correct in alerting us to the death drive of contemporary biopolitical commitments, es-pecially given the rise of the refugee and internment camp on a global scale. But the dialectics of life and death, visibility and invisibility, and privilege and lack in social existence that now constitute the biopolitics of modernity have to be understood in terms of their complexities, specificities, and diverse social forma-tions. For instance, the diverse ways in which the current articulation of biopower in the United States works to render some groups disposable and to privi-lege others within a permanent state of emergency need to be specified. Indeed, any viable rendering of contemporary biopolitics must address in detail how biopower functions not just to produce and control life in general, as Hardt and Negri insist, or, as Agamben argues, to reduce all inhabitants of the increasing militarized state to the dystopian space of the "death camp," but also to privilege *some* lives over others. The ongoing tragedy of pain and suffering wrought by the Bush administration's response to Hurricane Katrina reveals a biopolitical agenda in which the logic of disposability and the politics of death are inscribed differently in the order of contemporary power—structured largely around wretched and broad-based racial and class inequalities.

Just as crime in the existing order becomes a cultural attribute of the race- and class-specific other, disposability and death appear to be the unhappy lot of most powerless and marginalized social groups. "Broadly speaking, racism justifies the death-function in the economy of biopower," Foucault reminds us, "by appealing to the principle that the death of others makes one biologically stronger insofar as one is a member of a race or a population, insofar as one is an element in a unitary living plurality."[53] I want to further this position by arguing that neoliberalism, privatization, and militarism have become the dominant biopolitics of the mid-twentieth-century social state and that the coupling of a market fundamentalism and contemporary forms of subjugation of life to the power of capital accumulation, violence, and disposability, especially under the Bush administration, has produced a new and dangerous version of biopolitics.[54] While the murder of Emmett Till suggests that a biopolitics structured around the intersection of race and class inequalities, on the one hand, and state violence, on the other, is not new, the new version of biopolitics adds a distinctively different and more dangerous register to the older version of biopolitics. What is distinctive about the new form of biopolitics at work under the Bush administration is that it not only includes state-sanctioned violence but also relegates entire populations to spaces of invisibility and disposability. As William DiFazio points out, "the state has been so weakened over decades of privatization that it ... increasingly fails to provide health care, housing, retirement benefits and education to a massive percentage of its population."[55] While the social contract has been suspended in varying degrees since the 1970s, under the Bush administration it has been virtually abandoned. Under such circumstances, the state no longer feels obligated to take measures that prevent hardship, suffering, and death. The state no longer protects its own disadvantaged citizens—they are already seen as dead within the global economic/political framework. Specific populations now occupy a political space that effectively invalidates the categories of "citizen" and "democratic representation" that are integral to the nation-state system. In the past, people who were marginalized by class and race at least were supported by the government because of the social contract or because they still had some value as part of a reserve army of the unemployed. That is no longer true. This new form of biopolitics is conditioned by a permanent state of class and racial exception in which "vast populations are subject to conditions of life conferring upon them the status of living dead,"[56] largely invisible in the global media or, when disruptively present, defined as redundant, pathological, and dangerous. Within this wasteland of death and disposability, whole populations are relegated to what the sociologist Zygmunt Bauman calls "social homelessness."[57] While the rich and middle classes in the United States maintain lifestyles produced through vast inequalities of symbolic and material capital, the "free market" provides neither social protection, security, nor hope to those who are poor, sick, elderly, and marginalized by race and class. Given the increasingly perilous state of those who are poor and dispossessed in America, it is crucial to reexamine the ways in which biopower functions within global neoliberalism as well as the simultaneous rise of security states organized around cultural (and racial) homogeneity. This task is made all the more urgent by the destruction, politics, and death that followed Hurricane Katrina.[58]

Biopower and the Politics of Disposability

A blood-curdling thought: did not Katrina help, inadvertently, the efforts of the ailing disposal-industry of wasted humans, clearly not up to the task of coping with social consequences of the negative globalization of a crowded (and from the waste-disposal industry viewpoint, overcrowded) planet? Was not this help one of the reasons why the need to dispatch troops was not strongly felt until social order was broken and the prospect of social unrest came close?[59]

Biopower in its current shape has produced a new form of biopolitics marked by a cleansed visual and social landscape in which the poor, the elderly, the infirm, and criminalized populations share a common fate of disappearing from public view. Rendered invisible in deindustrialized communities far removed from the suburbs, barred from the tourist-laden sections of major cities, locked into understaffed nursing homes, interned in bulging prisons built in remote farm communities, hidden in decaying schools in rundown neighborhoods that bear the look of Third World slums, populations of poor black and brown citizens exist outside of the view of most Americans. They have become the waste-products of the American Dream, if not of modernity itself, as Zygmunt Bauman has argued for some time.[60] The disposable populations serve as an unwelcome reminder that the once-vaunted social state no longer exists, the living dead now an apt personification of the death of the social contract in the United States. Having fallen through the large rents in America's social safety nets, they reflect a governmental agenda bent on attacking the poor rather than attacking poverty. That they are largely poor and black undermines the nation's commitment to color-blind ideology; race remains the "major reason America treats its poor more harshly than any other advanced country."[61] One of the worst storms in our history shamed us into seeing the plight of poor blacks and other minorities. In less than forty-eight hours, Katrina ruptured the pristine image of America as a largely white, middle-class country modeled after a Disney theme park. Janet Pelz is right in arguing that Katrina showed us the murky quicksand beneath the Republican hype about the values and virtues of the alleged free market. She writes:

> Hurricane Katrina showed us faces the Republicans never wanted us to see—the elderly, the infirm, the poor. The ones with no car to get them out of the city before the storm hit, the ones unable to pay for hotel rooms until the waters receded. The ones with no health insurance to recover from the ravages of insulin shock, kidney failure or dehydration. The ones lying face down in the cesspool or dying of heatstroke in the Superdome.... As long as the poor remained out of sight, they could be described in whatever undeserving light the Republicans chose, and the rest of us would be unwilling to challenge them. This second Bush administration was to be the conservatives' crowning glory. They would finish slicing government to the bone, sacrificing environmental protections, critical infrastructure investments, health and human services, all to

massive tax cuts. Yes, the long climb back from the precipice of the New Deal was within reach. That is, until the poor came out of hiding and shamed us into seeing them. The [neoliberals] had sold us their theory—each of us should take care of ourselves. Citizens (at least those morally upstanding enough to be wealthy) could do better for ourselves than the government could do for us.[62]

Underneath neoliberalism's corporate ethic and market-based fundamentalism, not only is the idea of democracy disappearing but the spaces in which democracy is produced and nurtured are being eliminated. Democratic values, identities, and social relations along with public space, the common good, and the obligations of civic responsibility are slowly being overtaken by a market-based notion of freedom and civic indifference in which it becomes more difficult to translate private woes into social issues and collective action or to insist on a language of the public good. The upshot to this evisceration of all notions of sociality is a sense of total abandonment, resulting in fear, anxiety, and insecurity over one's future. The presence of the racialized poor, their needs, and their vulnerabilities—now visible—becomes unbearable. All solutions as a result now focus on shoring up a diminished sense of safety, carefully nurtured by a renewed faith in all things military.

The dangerous confluence of the war on terrorism, the culture of fear, and the pervasive influence of a growing militarism has "injected a constant military presence into our lives."[63] Militaristic values and military solutions are profoundly influencing every aspect of American life, ranging from foreign and domestic policy to the shaping of popular culture and the organization of public schools.[64] Military might becomes the highest expression of national greatness, and "war and warriors ... become the last, enduring symbols of American dominance and the American way of life."[65] Faith in democratic governance and cultural pluralism increasingly gives way to military-style uniformity, discipline, and authority coupled with a powerful nationalism and a stifling patriotic correctness, all of which undermine the force of a genuine democracy by claiming that the average citizen does not have the knowledge or authority to see, engage, resist, protest, or make dominant power accountable.[66]

With the loss of public space, it becomes difficult to either acknowledge, produce, or act on those principles, representations, and narratives of democracy that make hope and justice possible. In its place has emerged what Nicholas Mirzoeff calls the modern antispectacle. According to Mirzoeff, "the modern antispectacle now dictates that there is nothing to see and that instead one must keep moving, keep circulating and keep consuming."[67] Non-stop images coupled with a manufactured culture of fear strip citizens of their visual agency and potential to act as engaged social participants. Hence, it becomes more difficult for the engaged citizen "to attain the full authority of the visual subject, a person who is allowed to and required to look in all circumstances."[68] The visual subject has been reduced to the life-long consumer, always on the go looking for new goods and promising discounts, all the while traveling in spaces which suggest that public space is largely white and middle-class, free of both unproductive consumers and those individuals marked by the trappings of race, poverty, dependence, and disability. Hurricane Katrina broke through the visual blackout of poverty, low-income blacks, and the pernicious ideology of color-blindness to reveal the ineptness of the government's response efforts and the dire conditions of largely poor African-Americans, who were bearing the hardships incurred by the full wrath of the indifference and violence at work in the racial state.

One of the most obvious lessons of Katrina—that race and racism still matter in America—is fully operational through a biopolitics in which "sovereignty resides in the power and capacity to dictate who may live and who may die."[69] Katrina revealed not only how white America historically has felt about black cities and spaces—viewed more like colonial outposts that require a constant military presence—but also how such racist ideologies have translated into forms of underinvestment, criminalization, and a brutal lack of compassion on the part of the racial state. In the aftermath of Hurricane Katrina, the biopolitical calculus of massive power differentials and iniquitous market relations put the scourge of poverty and racism on full display.

Under the logic of modernization, neoliberalism, and militarization, the category "waste" includes no longer simply material goods but also human beings, particularly those rendered redundant in the new global economy—that is, those who are no longer capable of making a living, who are unable to consume goods, and who depend upon others for the most basic needs.[70] As the institutions of the welfare state along with "big government"—a code word for the social state—are deemed inefficient and wasteful by market fundamentalists and are either dismantled or phased out, those populations considered dependent and possessing no positive cultural capital or social role are increasingly viewed as an unwarranted burden to neoliberal society and left unprotected. As William

Greider points out, "what the Right is really seeking is not so much to be left alone by government but to use government to reorganize society in its own right-wing image."[71] Defined primarily through the combined discourses of character, personal responsibility, and cultural homogeneity, entire populations expelled from the benefits of the marketplace are reified as products without any value, to be disposed of as "leftovers in the most radical and effective way: we make them invisible by not looking and unthinkable by not thinking."[72] The protective functions of the state no longer apply to poor black and brown populations. In the new security state, such functions are primarily provided for the rich and the white middle class. Even when young black and brown youth try to escape the biopolitics of disposability by joining the military, the seduction of economic security is quickly negated by the horror of senseless violence compounded daily in the streets, roads, and battlefields in Iraq and Afghanistan and made concrete in the form of body bags, mangled bodies, and amputated limbs—rarely to be seen in the narrow ocular scope of the dominant media.

Biopolitics in its currently brutalizing neoliberal form inscribes into its power relations the logic of redundancy and disposability in order to eliminate all vestiges of the social contract, the welfare state, and any other public sphere not governed by the logic of profit or amenable to the imperatives of consumerism. With the social state in retreat and the rapacious dynamics of neoliberalism unchecked by government regulations, the public and private policies of investing in the public good are dismissed as bad business, just as the notion of protecting people from the dire misfortunes of poverty, sickness, or the random blows of fate is viewed as an act of bad faith. Weakness is now a sin, punishable by social exclusion. This is especially true for those racial groups and immigrant populations who have always been at risk economically and politically. Increasingly, such groups have become part of an ever-growing army of the impoverished and disenfranchised—removed from the prospect of a decent job, productive education, adequate health care, acceptable child-care services, and satisfactory shelter. As the state is transformed into one of the primary agents of terror and corporate concerns displace democratic values, official "power is measured by the speed with which responsibilities can be escaped."[73] With its pathological disdain for social values and public life and its celebration of unbridled individualism and acquisitiveness, the Bush administration does more than undermine the nature of social obligation and civic responsibility: It sends a message to those populations who are poor and black—society neither wants, cares about, nor needs you.[74] Katrina revealed with startling and disturbing clarity who these individuals are: African-Americans who occupy the poorest sections of New Orleans, those ghettoized frontier-zones created by racism coupled with economic inequality, which designate and constitute a "production line of human waste or wasted humans."[75] Cut out of any long-term goals and decent vision of the future, these are the populations, as Zygmunt Bauman points out, who have been rendered redundant and disposable in the age of neoliberal global capitalism. He writes:

> To be declared redundant means to have been disposed of because of being disposable—just like the empty and non-refundable plastic bottle or once-used syringe, an unattractive commodity with no buyers, or a substandard stained product without use thrown off the assembly line by the

quality inspectors. "Redundancy" shares its se-
mantic space with "rejects," "wastrels," "garbage,"
"refuse"—with *waste.* The destination of the unemployed, of the "reserve army of labour," was to
be called back into active service. The destination
of waste is the waste-yard, the rubbish heap....
"Organized society" treats them as "scroungers
and intruders," charges them at best with unwarranted pretenses or indolence, often with all
sorts of wickedness, like scheming, swindling,
living a life hovering on the brink of criminality,
but in each case with feeding parasitically on the
social body.... The superfluous are not just an
alien body, but a cancerous growth gnawing at
the healthy tissues of society and sworn enemies
of "our way of life" and "what we stand for."[76]

Katrina revealed a biopolitics in which the social contract has become obsolete and democratic governance
dysfunctional. It also made visible many of the social
mechanisms that render some populations disposable,
spatially fixed, and caught in a liminal space of uncertainty that not only limits choices but prioritizes for such
groups the power of death over life itself. In the case of
Katrina, a poisonous biopolitics was revealed in which
entire populations were "rendered invisible with the goal
of having them forgotten."[77] In Katrina's aftermath, the
entire world was exposed to a barrage of images in which
the poor black and brown populations appeared as
"waste turned out in ever rising volumes in our times."[78]
Instead of living in a world of consumer fantasies and
super-mall choices, these groups are caught in an existence filled with the nightmares of being left behind,
criminalized, and consequently charged with the guilt
of their exclusion, and left to fend for themselves (or die)
in the abandoned space of the urban ghetto, all created

by a neoliberal and racial state governed by a culture of economic efficiency, insecurity, ethical disengagement, surveillance, and manufactured cynicism.

In the following section, I want to be more specific about how the mechanisms of the neoliberal and racial state were at work in the unfolding of Hurricane Katrina. At stake here is the attempt to go beyond traditional explanations of the inadequacy of the Bush administration to deal with domestic catastrophes, the incompetence of specific individuals in positions of leadership, the aberrant natural forces beyond government control and accountability, or the dismal leadership of George W. Bush. Biopolitics under neoliberalism is informed by a particular vision of politics, government, public service, and the social contract—a vision that was on full display in the aftermath of Katrina. It is this set of issues that I want to explore.

Neoliberalism in Dark Times

Gone is any official speak of egalitarian futures, work for all, or the paternal government envisioned by the various freedom movements. These ideals have given way to a spirit of deregulation, with its taunting mix of emancipation and limitation. Individual citizens, a lot of them marooned by a rudderless ship of state, try to clamber aboard the good ship enterprise.... In this vocabulary, it is not just that the personal is political. The personal is the only politics there is, the only politics with a tangible referent or emotional valence. It is in these privatized terms that action is organized, that the experience of inequity and antagonism takes meaningful shape.[79]

In a May 25, 2001, interview, Grover Norquist, head of the right-wing group Americans for Tax Reform, told National Public Radio's Mara Liasson: "I don't want to abolish government. I simply want to reduce it to the size where I can drag it into the bathroom and drown it in the bathtub."[80] As a radical right-wing activist and practical strategist, labeled by Paul Gigot in the *Wall Street Journal* as the "V. I. Lenin of the anti-tax movement,"[81] Norquist got his wish in August 2005, and then some. He has been enormously instrumental and successful in shaping tax policies designed to "starve the beast," a metaphor for deliberate policies designed to drive up deficits by cutting taxes, especially for the rich, in order to paralyze government and dry up funds for many federal programs that offer protection for children, the elderly, and the poor. Norquist saw his efforts pay off when over sixteen hundred people, most of them poor and black, drowned in the basin of New Orleans and upwards of one million were displaced. As Ruth Conniff points out:

> These starving and drowning metaphors should give Americans pause as we look at New Orleans. The real human cost of the dismantling of civil society is on graphic display there. Siphoning money away from emergency relief, sending 35 percent of Louisiana's National Guard to tend to Bush's folly in Iraq, remaking the infrastructure of "homeland security" so its focus is on high-profile military and antiterrorist missions, and the basic job of defending our country from disaster—whether natural or manmade—goes by the boards—these are the hallmarks of this Administration. And the idea that somehow government, except for the military, is bad, and huge tax cuts and the resulting cuts in federal spending are good, has helped get us where we are today.[82]

The neoliberal efforts to shrink big government and public services must be understood both in terms of those who bore the brunt of such efforts in New Orleans and in terms of the subsequent inability of the government to deal adequately with Hurricane Katrina. Reducing the federal government's ability to respond to social problems is a decisive element of neoliberal policymaking, as was echoed in a *Wall Street Journal* editorial that argued without irony that taxes should be raised for low-income individuals and families not to make more money available to the federal government for addressing their needs but to rectify the possibility that they "might not be feeling a proper hatred for the government."[83] If the poor can be used as pawns in this logic to further the political attack on big government, it seems reasonable to assume that those in the Bush administration who hold such a position would refrain from using big government as quickly as possible to save the very lives of such groups, as was evident in the aftermath of Katrina. The vilification of big government—really an attack on nonmilitary aspects of government designed to regulate the market—has translated into a steep decline of tax revenues, a massive increase in military spending, and the growing immiseration of poor Americans and people of color. Under the Bush administration, Census Bureau figures reveal "that since 1999, the income of the poorest fifth of Americans has dropped 8.7 percent in inflation-adjusted dollars ... [and in 2005] 1.1 million were added to the 36 million already on the poverty rolls."[84] While the number of Americans living below the poverty line is comparable to the combined populations of Louisiana, Mississippi, Alabama, Texas, and Arkansas, the Bush administration chose to include in the 2006 budget $70 billion in new tax cuts for the rich while slashing programs that benefit the least fortunate.[85] Similarly, the projected $2.7 trillion budget for 2007 includes a $4.9 billion reduction in health funds for senior citizens (Medicare) and the State Children's Health Insurance Program; a $17 million cut in aid for child-support enforcement; cutbacks in funds for low-income people with disabilities; major reductions in Child Care and Development Block Grants; major defunding for housing for low-income elderly; and an unprecedented rollback in student aid. In addition, the 2007 budget calls for another $70 billion dollars in tax cuts that are most beneficial to the rich and provide for a huge increase in military spending for the war in Iraq.[86]

Poverty and inequality take a tragic toll on the young, poor, illiterate, elderly, and predominantly people of color, and the consequences are seldom seen on television. To be born poor in the United States means that in some cases children have to pay with their lives. Hence, it comes as no surprise, as *New York Times* reporter Nicholas D. Kristof observes,

> that the infant mortality rate in America's capital is twice as high as in China's capital. That's right—the number of babies who died before their first birthdays amounted to 11.5 per thousand live births in 2002 in Washington, compared with 4.6 in Beijing.... [Moreover,] under Bush, the national infant mortality rate has risen for the first time since 1958. The U.S. ranks 43rd in the world in infant mortality and nationally 29% of kids had no health insurance at some point in the last 12 months, and many get neither checkups nor vaccinations. On immunizations, the U.S. ranks 84th for measles and 89th for polio.[87]

While President Bush endlessly argues for the economic benefits of his tax cuts, he callously omits the fact that 13 million children are living in poverty in the United States, "4.5 million more than when Bush was first inaugurated."[88] And New Orleans has the third highest rate of children living in poverty in the United States.[89] The illiteracy rate in New Orleans before the flood struck was 40 percent; the embarrassingly ill-equipped public school system was one of the most underfunded in the nation. Nearly 19 percent of Louisiana residents lacked health insurance, putting the state near the bottom for the percentage of people without health insurance. Robert Scheer, a journalist and social critic, estimates that one-third of the 150,000 people living in dire poverty were elderly, left exposed to the flooding in areas most damaged by Katrina.[90] It gets worse. In an ironic twist of fate, one day after Katrina hit New Orleans, the U.S. Census Bureau released two important reports on poverty indicating showed that "Mississippi (with a 21.6 percent poverty rate) and Louisiana (19.4 percent) are the nation's poorest states, and that New Orleans (with a 23.2 percent poverty rate) is the 12th poorest city in the nation. [Moreover,] New Orleans is not only one of the nation's poorest cities, but its poor people are among the most concentrated in poverty ghettos. Housing discrimination and the location of government subsidized housing have contributed to the city's economic and racial segregation."[91] Under neoliberal capitalism, the attack on politically responsible government has only been matched by an equally harsh attack on social provisions and safety nets for the poor.

Lewis Lapham argues that under the Bush administration, government has become "a trailer park for deadbeats who can't afford to hire their own servants, furnish their own police protection, hire cheap Chinese labor, [or] pay their taxes in Bermuda."[92] And despite the massive failures of market-driven neoliberal policies—ranging from a soaring $420 billion budget deficit to the underfunding of schools, public health, community policing, and environmental protection programs—the reigning right-wing orthodoxy of the Bush administration continues to "give precedence to private financial gain and market determinism over human lives and broad public values."[93] As David Theo Goldberg observes, private interests now trump public needs and largely benefit those who are wealthy, white, and aligned with the Bush administration:

> Privatizing the conditions of well-being has meant the wealthy have the best medical care while the multitude have none. The well-off live in gated communities high on the hill while the poor live in polluted neighborhoods vulnerably below sea level with no garbage collection and few options. The powerful drive larger and larger gas-guzzling SUVs while the impoverished have no public transportation to speak of. The newly rich drink imported bottled water while the struggling have only polluted tap water. One in seven people in the U.S. have no medical insurance today, and one in eight now live in poverty. In New Orleans those figures are closer to one quarter. The wealthy can dine daily in restaurants while the poor barely have anything to eat at all, and can afford nothing by the end of each month as they await pay checks or welfare subsistence, or both. The wealthy get tax breaks and stock options while the poor can't even depend on the most rudimentary of educations. The lives of the rich are guarded from those of the poor whose fate is more likely prison than work.[94]

The Bush administration's ideological hostility toward the essential role that government should play in providing social services and crucial infrastructure was particularly devastating for New Orleans in the aftermath of Hurricane Katrina. Prior to 9/11, the Federal Emergency Management Agency listed a hurricane strike on New Orleans as one of the three most likely catastrophic disasters facing America. The *Houston Chronicle* wrote in December 2001 that "[t]he New Orleans hurricane scenario may be the deadliest of all."[95] And yet the Bush administration consistently denied repeated requests for funds by the New Orleans Army Corps of Engineers. Ignoring such requests, the Bush administration cut the Army Corps' funding by more than a half-billion dollars in its 2002 budget, leaving unfinished the construction for levees that eventually burst. And they did so during the "same year that the richest 5 percent (those who make an average of $300,000) were slated to receive $24 billion in new tax cuts."[96] Huge tax cuts for the rich and massive cuts in much-needed social programs continued unabated in the Bush administration, all the while putting the lives of thousands of poor people in the Gulf Basin in jeopardy. In spite of repeated warnings far in advance by experts that the existing levees could not withstand a Category 4 hurricane, the Bush administration in 2004 rejected the Southeast Louisiana Urban Flood Control Project's request for $100 million, offering instead a measly $16.5 million. As David Sirota has reported, such funds were to be used "to strengthen the levees holding back the Mississippi River and Lake Pontchartrain. *The Chicago Tribune* noted that the Army Corps of Engineers had also requested $27 million to pay for hurricane protection upgrades around Lake Pontchartrain—but the White House pared that back to $3.9 million. Meanwhile, budget cuts forced the corps to delay seven projects that included enlarging critical levees."[97] As Sirota further observes, this disastrous underfunding of efforts to build the levee infrastructure, coupled with even more tax cuts for the rich and less revenue for the states, continued right up to the time that Hurricane Katrina struck, making it almost impossible for governments in the Gulf region either to protect their citizens from the impact of a major hurricane or to develop the resources necessary for an adequate emergency response plan in the event of a flood. Sirota writes:

> The weeks and months leading up to Hurricane Katrina were more of the same. The White house focused on a multi-trillion-dollar plan to privatize Social Security, and a plan to repeal the federal estate tax. Meanwhile, as the *Financial Times* reported, the President proposed a budget that "called for a $71.2 million reduction in federal funding for hurricane and flood prevention projects in the New Orleans district, the largest such cut ever proposed." In addition, "the administration wanted to shelve a study aimed at determining ways to protect New Orleans from a Category 5 hurricane." This, in the face of a March 2005 report by the American Society of Civil Engineers that warned 3,500 dams were at risk of failing unless the government spent $10 billion to fix them.[98]

President Bush did not address questions about the lack of proper funding for the levees. Instead, he played dumb and, in spite of overwhelming evidence to the contrary, came up with one of the most incredible soundbites of his career: "I don't think anyone anticipated the breach of the levees."[99] In fact, Bush was briefed the day before Katrina hit and emphatically warned by a number of disaster officials that the levees could breach—a position Bush, of course, later denied.[100] Much of the press viewed Bush's remarks about the levees as indicative of a president who was simply clueless and indifferent to any information that did not conform to his own budget-busting, anti–big government ideology. For instance, Mike Allen, writing in *Time* magazine, implied that Bush's circle of advisers has become increasingly hermetic, "with fewer people willing to bring him bad news." He then tells the story about a young aide who "as a Bush favorite described the perils of correcting the boss: 'The first time I told him he was wrong, he started yelling at me,' the aide recalled about a session during the first term. 'Then I showed him where he was wrong, and he said, "All right, I understand. Good job." He patted me on the shoulder. I went and had dry heaves in the bathroom.'"[101] As instructive as this story is, it says nothing about a failure of leadership and governance based on the assumption that being inattentive to "bad news" is justified because such news often derives from issues that directly affect those populations marginalized by poverty, unemployment, and racism. Such political and moral indifference is linked less to narrow-mindedness and a rigidity of character than it is to a set of biopolitical commitments that dictate who lives and who dies in the context of a rabid neoliberalism and a morally bankrupt neoconservatism.[102] But it is more than this still. The government's failure to respond quickly to the black poor on the Gulf Coast can be related to a deeper set of memories of racial injustice and violence, memories that suggest a link between an apartheid past and the present intensification of its utter disregard for populations now considered disposable. Michael Eric Dyson elaborates on this in his analysis of the Katrina disaster. He writes:

The black poor of the Delta lacked social standing, racial status, and the apparent and uncon-
scious identifiers that might evoke a dramatic
empathy in Bush and Brown. Had these factors
been present, it might have spurred Bush and
Brown to identify *with* the black poor, indeed, see
themselves *as* the black poor. Since their agency
and angst had been minimized in the Southern
historical memory, the black poor simply didn't
register as large, or count as much, as they
might have had they been white. If they had been
white, a history of identification—supported by
structures of care, sentiments of empathy, and
an elevated racial standing—would have immediately kicked in. That might have boosted con-
siderably their chances of survival because the
federal government, including Bush and Brown,
would have seen their kind, perhaps their kin,
and hence themselves, floating in a flood of death
in the Delta.[103]

The Biopolitics of Poverty and Race

[A]nd for all that poor blacks have experienced
and endured in this country, they had good reason to be surprised that they were treated not
as citizens but as garbage.... They know they
live in an unjust and unfair society.... So it is
not—as some commentators claimed—that the
catastrophe laid bare the deep inequalities of
American society. These inequalities may have
been news to some, but they were not news to
the displaced people in the convention center
and elsewhere. What was bitter news to them
was that their claims of citizenship mattered

so little to the institutions charged with their protection.[104]

Soon after Hurricane Katrina hit the Gulf Coast, the consequences of the long legacy of attacking big government and bleeding the social support and public service sectors of the state became glaringly evident. The "Other America," afflicted by rank poverty, deeply rooted racism, and abject suffering, was exposed live and in living color on television screens all over the world. What was also revealed—besides large groups of people stranded on highways crying out for help, corpses propped up in wheelchairs, and bloated bodies floating in the rancid floodwaters of New Orleans for weeks on end—was a government that displayed a "dangerous incompetence and ... staggering indifference to human suffering."[105] James Carroll writing in the *Boston Globe* argued that Katrina was more than simply a natural disaster; it was a "political epiphany" that revealed the fatal consequences of stripping government of its civic functions. He writes:

> The spectacle of failure, how for days the government was powerless to help such people, only put on display how government was already failing them and everyone else.... [W]hat it means is that the United States, after a generation of tax-cutting and downsizing, has eviscerated the public sector's capacity for supporting the common good. The neglect of civic infrastructure, the destruction of social services, the abandonment of the safety net, the myth of "privatization," the perverse idea, dating [back] to the Reagan era, that government is the enemy: it all adds up to what we saw last week—government not as the enemy, but as the incompetent, impotent bystander. The bystander-

in-chief, of course, is George W. Bush, whose whining self-obsession perfectly embodies what America had done to itself.[106]

Hurricane Katrina made it abundantly clear that only the government had the power, resources, and authority to address complex undertakings such as dealing with the totality of the economic, environmental, cultural, and social destruction that impacted the Gulf Coast. It also revealed that the Bush administration was incapable of either the leadership or the willingness to bring the federal government's resources—or whatever resources it could muster after tax cuts and a costly war—to bear on such a catastrophic problem. But the problem went much deeper. Given the Bush administration's disdain for the legacy of the New Deal, important government agencies were viewed scornfully as oversized entitlement programs, stripped of their power, and served up as a dumping ground to provide lucrative administrative jobs for political hacks who were often unqualified to lead such agencies. As is well known, the most blatant example can be found in the Bush administration's eagerness to erode the capacity of the Federal Emergency Management Agency for dealing with major disasters. Not only was FEMA downsized and placed under the Department of Homeland Security, but its role in disaster planning and preparation was subordinated to the all-inclusive goal of fighting terrorists. The two directors appointed by President Bush were political cronies who had no experience in disaster management. The first, Joe Albaugh, had no relevant qualifications other than being a chief Bush political operative for years. Similarly, the second director, Michael Brown, got the job simply because he was part of the old-boy network, and his only qualification for the job was as a commissioner for the International Arabian Horse Association, which fired him for "supervision failures." Even when it had become clear a few days after Katrina hit the Gulf Coast that Brown was bungling the hurricane response effort, Bush supported him, stating on a national televised news broadcast, "Brownie, you're doing a heck of a job," only to eventually ask him to resign several weeks later.

But FEMA was far from alone in failing to respond adequately and quickly to Hurricane Katrina. The government neither put in place adequate evacuation plans, even though Katrina came with two days warning, nor provided transportation for people who lacked money, cars, or help to get them out of the city. Trucks filled with ice were routed to different states outside of the Gulf Coast. As Terry Lynn Karl points out, "there were not enough facilities to house and care for refugees, there were not forces in place to deliver desperately needed supplies or to secure order, and nowhere near the number of boats and helicopters and other craft necessary to reach the stranded.... For four days, there was simply no clear center of command and control. As a result, countless people suffered and died."[107] When evacuation efforts were finally in place, thousands of displaced hurricane victims were sent off to other states without being told where they were being relocated. Months after Katrina, hundreds of displaced citizens failed to receive any of the thousands of trailers that stood idle and decaying in farmlands in other states; bodies lay unclaimed in destroyed houses; and many people whose homes were destroyed, especially those in the poorer sections, were still waiting for any sign of relief from the government.

In February 2006, thousands of evacuees dispersed across the country were forced from their hotels when the federal government stopped paying their bills. Some of them received further rental assistance, but many had no place to go. Others found that the rental assistance was not enough to rent rooms. Some of the evacuees returning to New Orleans had been given housing vouchers when first shipped to Houston, Texas, but discovered that the vouchers were not honored in New Orleans.[108] All the while, 10,777 new mobile homes provided by FEMA were sinking in the Arkansas mud, unusable and costing American taxpayers $850 million and still counting.[109] As of this writing, six months after Katrina, dozens of unrecovered bodies remain in the largely black Ninth Ward, but FEMA has still not allocated money to get the rescue operations moving again.[110] Black bodies, it seems, can simply be relegated to the status of human waste, outside of the protective services of the state, outside of the moral compass of justice, reduced to rotting along with the houses destroyed by the flood.

A congressional report released by a committee staffed entirely by Republicans claims that Katrina was a national failure and that FEMA head Michael Brown and Homeland Security Secretary Michael Chertoff were detached and clueless. According to the 600–page-plus report, Katrina "was a failure of leadership": the White House did not "substantiate, analyze and act on the information at its disposal . . . [and] Katrina was a national failure, an abdication of the most solemn obligation to provide the common welfare."[111] And yet, while it was virtually impossible to miss the failure of the government response to Katrina, what many people saw as incompetence or a failure of national leadership was more than that. Godfrey Hodgson rightly argues that while incompetence and failure of leadership cannot be discounted in understanding the government response to Hurricane

Katrina, the explanation for failure lies elsewhere. He claims "[I]t is to be found in the callous indifference among conservatives towards the poor.... [I]t was nevertheless an absence of sympathy, not a lack of means, which motivated the low priority given to poor, mostly black victims."[112] In this instance, matters of sympathy aside, something more systemic and deep-rooted was revealed in the wake of Katrina—namely, that a decades-long official policy of *benign* neglect had become *malign* neglect.

Denying that the federal government alone had the resources to address catastrophic events, the Bush administration was not simply unprepared for Hurricane Katrina: It actually felt no responsibility for the lives of poor blacks and others marginalized by poverty and relegated to the outskirts of society. Former British Prime Minister Margaret Thatcher's famous declaration that "there is no such thing as society. There are individual men and women, and there are families. And no government can do anything except through people, and people must look to themselves first"[113] has become the quintessential neoliberal rationalization for dismantling social subjects and social bonds as well as liquidating the gains of the welfare state.[114] Thatcher was simply echoing a central tenet of neoliberal policy that would dominate U.S. policy from the middle of the 1970s up to the new millennium. Attempting to undo the legacy and policies of the New Deal and the Great Society, advocates of neoliberalism from Ronald Reagan to Bill Clinton have made a concerted effort to roll back the social welfarist commitments central to an inclusive democracy. This has meant reversing the long-standing assumption that officials from all levels of government should assume a large measure of responsibility for providing the resources, social provisions, and modes of education for their citizens, especially the young, the poor, immigrants, and people of color—in short, those groups generally excluded from the operations of power, symbolic and material capital, and the realm of politics. Biopolitics took a deadly turn with the election of George W. Bush in 2004. Bush and his neoliberal and neoconservative cronies considered the social contract dangerous because it set limits to the reign of the "free market" and was premised on the idea that the state should ensure each of its citizens equal opportunity in life and should play a major role in protecting everyone from life's hazards—unemployment, growing old, and getting sick, among others.

Under the administration of George W. Bush, biopolitics was stripped of any commitment to social justice and an obligation to future generations. Democracy's ideals took a hit as success was now measured in short-term financial gains; the market was universalized and served as a model to cover all human relationships; profit became the most important measure of national well-being and security; all values were now determined by economic criteria; and the corporate elite and the wealthy aggressively altered government to serve their own narrow interests. Intervention by the government on behalf of its citizens against life's hardships and in support of the larger public good was now viewed as the enemy of a market-based notion of democracy. For this new generation of market fundamentalists, the idea, not to mention the reality, of justice seemed dead on arrival as it drained from the public treasury billions of dollars through tax cuts for the rich and allocated huge appropriations for a bloated military budget while aggressively enacting retrograde policies that seem intent on increasing corporate power and wasting billions of dollars on a rapacious and deadly empire-building fiasco in Iraq.

Equally important, as the nation-state was transformed into the market state,[115] it became clear that the role of the state was to generate financial rewards and privileges for only some members of society, while the welfare of those marginalized by race and class was now viewed with criminal contempt. The coupling of the market state with the racial state under George W. Bush meant that policies would be aggressively pursued to dismantle the welfare state, eliminate affirmative action, model urban public schools after prisons, aggressively pursue anti-immigrant policies, and incarcerate with impunity Arabs, Muslims, and poor youth of color.

Society no longer comprised just individuals and families, as Thatcher claimed, but was inhabited exclusively by white individuals and families as it developed into a space increasingly cleansed of immigrants and those who were black, brown, and poor—that is, all those groups seen as both expendable and potentially threatening to a consumer-happy and racially homogenous social order. The question no longer seemed to be whether the government had an obligation to help those suffering from the harsh realities of economic misfortune and the overbearing vulnerabilities produced in a society marked by deep social, racial, and economic inequalities. On the contrary, the central commitment of the new biopolitics of hyper-neoliberalism was now organized around the best way to remove or make invisible those individuals and groups who were either a drain on or stood in the way of market freedoms, free trade, consumerism, and the neoconservative dream of an American empire. According to the new biopolitics of disposability, the poor, especially people of color, not only had to fend for themselves in the face of life's tragedies but were also supposed to do it without being seen by the dominant society. Excommunicated from the sphere of human concern, they had been rendered invisible, utterly disposable, and heir to that army of socially homeless that allegedly no longer existed in color-blind America.

How else to explain the cruel jokes and insults either implied or made explicit by Bush and his ideological allies in the aftermath of such massive destruction and suffering? When it became obvious in the week following Katrina that thousands of the elderly, poor, and sick could not get out of New Orleans because they had no cars or money to take a taxi or any other form of transportation, or were sick and infirm, the third-highest-ranking politician in Washington, Rick Santorum, stated in an interview "that people who did not heed evacuation warnings in the future may need to be penalized."[116] For Santorum, those who were trapped in the flood because of poverty, sickness, and lack of transportation had become an unwelcome reminder of the state of poverty and racism in the United States, and for that they should be punished. Their crime, it seems, was that a natural disaster made a social and politically embarrassing disaster visible to the world, and they just happened to be its victims. Commenting on facilities that had been set up for the poor in the Houston Astrodome in Texas, Bush's mother and the wife of former President George H. W. Bush said in a National Public Radio interview, "So many of the people here, you know, were underprivileged anyway, so this is working very well for them."[117] John Nichols, commenting on Barbara Bush's comments, writes: "On the tape of the interview, Mrs. Bush chuckles audibly as she observes just how great things are going for families that are separated from loved ones, people who have been forced to abandon their homes and the only community where they have ever lived, and parents who are explaining to children that their pets, their toys and in some cases their friends may be lost forever. Perhaps the former first lady was amusing herself with the notion that evacuees without bread could eat cake."[118] Other right-wing ideologues seeking to deflect criticism from the obscene incompetence and indifference of the Bush administration used a barely concealed racism to frame the events of Katrina. The cantankerous discourse of talk radio in America, which is almost exclusively right-wing, was quick to invoke racist fears and hate speech after the disaster struck. For example, Neil Boortz, a syndicated host on WFTL-AM in Florida, stated that "a huge percentage" of those forced to leave New Orleans were "parasites, like ticks on a dog. They are coming to a community near you."[119] Kelly Mitchell, who broadcasted for a week from the Houston Astrodome among flood victims, was obsessed with alleged looting by blacks in New Orleans, calling the state "Lose-iana." Entirely unreflective about her own racism, she referred to the victims who had lost family members and relatives in the flood this way: "If I heard, 'I'm looking for my mom, my dad, and my baby daddy again,' I would cringe. Everybody knows it's important to speak English but these knuckleheads."[120] But the general temper of such rabid expressions of old-time racism was not limited to the fringes of right-wing talk radio. On the September 13 broadcast of *The Radio Factor,* Fox News host Bill O'Reilly overtly indulged his own racism before millions of his viewers in claiming that poor black people in New Orleans were basically drug addicts who failed to evacuate the city because they would not have access to their fix. As O'Reilly put it:

> Now, our government has a duty to provide a safety net so these people aren't living under

bridges. But some of them are anyway, because all the entitlement money they get they spend on heroin or crack or alcohol. So they can't pay their rent because the money that they're given they spend on drugs and alcohol. So what do you do? Give them more money? They're not going to pay their rent, they're going to spend it on drugs and alcohol. And therefore, they're going to be out on the street with their hand out. Many, many, many of the poor in New Orleans are in that condition. They weren't going to leave no matter what you did. They were drug-addicted. They weren't going to get turned off from their source. They were thugs, whatever.[121]

Surviving a disaster like Katrina is easier for the rich than it is for the poor, especially for the 30 percent of New Orleans' residents who lived below the poverty line. O'Reilly seems to have forgotten that a privileged white man like himself could simply have driven out of New Orleans in his tanked-up SUV, but that was not true for the "134,000 people [who] couldn't leave because they couldn't afford transportation."[122]

In one of the most blatant displays of racism underscoring the biopolitical "live free or die" agenda in Bush's America, the dominant media increasingly framed the events that unfolded during and immediately after the hurricane by focusing on acts of crime, looting, rape, and murder, allegedly perpetrated by the black residents of New Orleans. The day after the levees broke, the Associated Press reported stories about massive looting, only to be followed by an endless stream of reports on Fox News, in the mainstream news media, and among right-wing bloggers about cases of rapes, murders, and looting by black people, even though such stories were unsubstantiated.[123]

Right-wing pundit and Fox News Channel contributor Michelle Malkin listed endless examples from other newspapers of looting and crime on her website, all woefully unsubstantiated, and argued that the chaos in New Orleans was strictly due to lawlessness.[124] Peggy Noonan, a contributing editor of the *Wall Street Journal,* openly insisted that looters be shot, a barely coded rationale to shoot low-income black people.[125] Repeatedly, local and national news outlets claimed that black people, both in the city and those trying to leave, were "bringing with them the worst of New Orleans's now-notorious lawlessness: looting, armed car jacking, and even the rape of children."[126] Rather than being viewed as victims of a disaster that pointed to the failure of a government to protect its citizens and take the social contract seriously, low-income blacks were increasingly portrayed as criminals. Rather than focus on the thousands of people who were injured, suffering, or just plain living in misery with little or no help, lacking both relief or the possibility of escape, the media chose to focus on fabricated stories about black deviance and pathology.

According to stories circulated widely in the media, low-income blacks were rioting in shelters; cars were being hijacked at gunpoint in New Orleans; riots were breaking out in Baton Rouge; looters were firing at helicopters; and a 7–year-old was raped in Houston's Astrodome. Later inquiries revealed that almost all of these crimes did not take place. Howard Witt, a writer for the *Chicago Tribune,* claimed that reports about an explosion of black violence in Baton Rouge simply were false. He writes: "The police, for example, confiscated a single knife from a refugee in one Baton Rouge shelter. . . . There were no riots in Baton Rouge. There were no armed hordes."[127] When Michael Chertoff was asked about looters shooting at helicopters, he replied: "I haven't actually received a confirmed report of someone firing on a helicopter."[128] Tim Wise wrote that some people who did see guns fired "report that it was intended to get the attention of the helicopters, which seemed to be repeatedly passing people by, looking at the catastrophic conditions, but refusing to land and save people in most instances.... Either way, the gunfire was a desperate attempt to get people to take things seriously and do their jobs: perhaps not the best way to get attention, but hardly the act of mindless, violent thugs aiming indiscriminately at everyone in sight, as reports made it seem."[129] Mike Davis and Anthony Fontenot interviewed a number of emergency-response workers in New Orleans, and they confirm a similar story. In an exchange with Vincent, one of the workers charged with the task of removing dead bodies, they reported the following:

> "We were under strict orders to remove only bodies. But there were still lots of people on the roofs or leaning out the windows of their houses. They were crazy with fear and thirst. They screamed, begged and cursed us. But we had a boatload of bodies, some probably infectious. So we saved the dead and left the living." Vincent believes that the "sniper activity" so luridly reported in the media was from stranded people who were outraged when boats and helicopters ignored them.[130]

I am not suggesting that some looting and thievery did not take place, especially when prompted by the necessity to forage for basic goods in order to survive; but certainly this is a reality very different from the claim that a total breakdown of law and order took place. When George Bush was asked by Diane Sawyer if a distinction should be drawn between people clearly looting and those taking goods necessary for survival, Bush replied, "it should be zero tolerance." In spite of Bush's claims to compassionate conservatism, this hard-line position is not surprising from a president whose policies have consistently punished the racialized poor.

The philosopher Slavoj Zizek argues that "what motivated these stories were not facts, but racist prejudices, the satisfaction felt by those who would be able to say: 'You see, Blacks really are like that, violent barbarians under the thin layer of civilization!'"[131] It must be noted that there is more at stake here than the resurgence of old-style racism; there is the recognition that some groups have the power to protect themselves from such stereotypes and other do not, and for those who do not—especially poor blacks—racist myths have a way of producing precise, if not deadly, material consequences. As Zizek points out, "These reports were not merely words, they were words that had material effects: They generated fears that caused some police officers to quit and led the authorities to change troop deployments, delay medical evacuations and ground helicopters. Acadian Ambulance company, for example, locked down its cars after word came that armed robbers had looted all of the water from a firehouse in Covington—a report that proved totally untrue."[132] Just as the dominant media and various racist groups who make up the anti-government Right had supported the Bush administration in attacking the safety net instead of poverty, these same groups were quick to ignore the grinding poverty, widespread homelessness, neglect, and failing schools that turned a natural disaster along the Gulf Coast into a social disaster that had to be analyzed within the context of a history of racist policies and governmental neglect. Given the public's preoccupation with violence and safety, crime and terror merge in the all-too-familiar equation of black culture with the culture of criminality, and images of poor blacks are made indistinguishable from images of crime and violence. Certainly racist stereotyping translates into the most retrograde policy in Louisiana, where deindustrialization, disinvestment, outsourcing, and downsizing have created a disposable population of black men who have to bear the brunt of the violence of a racial state. As Jordan Flaherty and Tamika Middleton point out, Louisiana has the highest rate of incarceration in the country—816 sentenced prisoners per 100,000 state residents.... Although Blacks make up 32 percent of Louisiana's population, they constitute 72 percent of the state's prison population.... Black men from New Orleans end up in Angola prison, a former slave plantation ... and over 90 percent of inmates eventually die in the prison."[133] Criminalizing black behavior and relying on punitive measures to solve social problems do more than legitimate a biopolitics defined increasingly by the authority of an expanding national security state under George W. Bush. They also legitimize a state in which the police and military, often operating behind closed doors, take on public functions that are not subject to public scrutiny.[134] This becomes particularly dangerous in a democracy when paramilitary or military organizations gain their legitimacy increasingly from an appeal to fear and terror, prompted largely by the presence of those racialized and class-specific groups considered both dangerous and disposable. Indeed, John and Jean Comaroff argue that racialized violence can be

> immensely productive, sometimes horrifyingly so; quite apart from its capacity to redirect the

flow of wealth, it usurps representation, reveals the limits of order, and justifies state monopolies over the means of coercion.... Violent crime ... has become the lightning rod for an escalating range of everyday anxieties—anxieties fed by the insecurity of the privileged as they witness the banal theatrics of the mass media; crime becomes radicalized and race criminalized.[135]

The metaphysics of disorder appears crucial in promoting the spectacle of militarization and policing, not only pandering to the everyday anxieties of the privileged but also, in the case of the Katrina tragedy, making sure that when race and disaster collide, the first casualty has to be the truth. But media panics mobilized around fictitious acts of racialized violence are never simply about the circulation of unfortunate stereotypes forged in the public imagination; they also often have terrible tangible effects, and such effects were on full display in the immediate aftermath of Katrina.

In the case of Katrina, low-income blacks, long the victims of retrograde federal policies, the hollowing out of the state, grinding poverty, and harsh treatment by the punishment industries, were thrust into full view of the world; and within a very short time, images of despair and human suffering were transformed into a monstrous spectacle that quickly passed from demonization to criminalization to militarization. Cries of desperation and help were quickly redefined as the pleas of "refugees," a designation which suggests that an alien force lacking both citizenship and legal rights had inhabited the Gulf Coast. Also within a short time, victims were branded in the media as looters and thugs. In predictable fashion, politicians such as Louisiana Governor Kathleen Blanco issued an order allowing soldiers to shoot to kill looters in an effort to restore calm. Commenting on the media's role in demonizing the poverty-stricken victims of Katrina and the increasingly militaristic response to those victims, James Petras wrote: "Washington's 'Shoot to Kill' order applied to water bottle snatchers and the real or imagined snipers. Negative labelling of the victims by the media heightened the public's distrust of the testimonials of dehydrated children and frail grandmothers. Criminalization, demonization, and militarization [are] what Washington does best."[136]

Within a few days, New Orleans was under martial law occupied by nearly 65,000 U.S. military personnel. Images of thousands of desperate and poor blacks gave way to pictures of squads of combat-ready troops and soldiers with mounted bayonets canvassing houses in order to remove stranded civilians. Embedded journalists now traveled with soldiers on Humvees, armored carriers, and military helicopters in downtown U.S.A. What had begun as a botched rescue operation by the federal government was transformed into a military operation. Brian Williams, reporting on MSNBC, commented that "[i]t is impossible to over-emphasize the extent to which this area [New Orleans] is under government occupation, and portions of it under government-enforced lockdown. Police cars rule the streets."[137]

Given the government's propensity to view those who are poor and black with contempt, it is not surprising that the transformation of New Orleans and the Gulf Coast from disaster area to war zone occurred without any audible dissent from either the general public or the dominant media. New Orleans increasingly came to look like a city in Iraq as scores of private soldiers appeared on the scene—either on contract with the Department of Homeland Security or hired by wealthy elites to protect their private estates and businesses. Just as the occupation of Iraq has been privatized with thousands of private military contractors occupying the country, New Orleans became another recipient of deregulated militarized market capitalism as soon as the flood waters began to recede. According to Jeremy Scahill, "mercenaries from companies like DynCorp, Intercon, American Security Group, Blackhawk, Wackenhut and an Israeli company called Instinctive Shooting International [fanned] out to guard private businesses and homes, as well as government projects and institutions. Within two weeks of the hurricane, the number of private security companies registered in Louisiana jumped from 185 to 235."[138] The fruits of privatization and an utter disregard for public values are all too visible in the use of private mercenaries and security companies hired to guard federal projects, often indulging in acts of violence that constitute a clear-cut case of vigilantism. Michael Ratner, president of the Center for Constitutional Rights, brought this point home when he observed that "[t]his vigilantism demonstrates the utter breakdown of the government. These private security forces have behaved brutally, with impunity, in Iraq. To have them now on the streets of New Orleans is frightening and possibly illegal."[139]

The militarization of New Orleans goes hand in hand with a biopolitics that subordinates human needs to profit and democracy to the dictates of capital and authoritarian control. Profits, consumerism, and privatization have become the holy trinity of a market fundamentalism driving the recovery efforts in the Gulf Coast. The armed forces did more than restore order in New Orleans; they also provided the advance guard for cleansing the city of its largely black population while opening up exciting new investment opportunities for corporations, increased capital investment, and soaring financial gains. The army and police forces not only forced residents to leave their property; they also dispersed them throughout the United States. Once low-income blacks had left the city, political and corporate leaders were quick to envision a rebuilt New Orleans as a very different city. Speaker of the House Dennis Hastert suggested that much of New Orleans should be bulldozed, indicating that "the best way to fix the persistent problem of poverty in New Orleans is simply make it too hard for poor people to live there. Baton Rouge's Representative Baker suggested that the hurricane did the hard work of cleaning up low income housing for him."[140] James Rice, a local businessman, told the *Wall Street Journal:* "Those who want to see this city rebuilt want to see it done in a completely different way, *demographically,* geographically and politically. I am not just speaking for myself here. The way we have been living is not going to happen again or we're out" (emphasis added).[141]

Recovery efforts in the Gulf Coast raise a fundamental question of governance in a democratic society: What are the government's obligations to society, to its citizens as citizens? And the answer that has emerged from the Bush administration suggests that none exists. The twin logics of economic investment, on the one hand, and disposability, on the other, are based on privileging corporations, markets, privatization, and empire-building over people, especially those who are immigrants, lack power and wealth, and are nonwhite. Instead of billions flowing to the poor who have lost their jobs, homes, and dignity, the Bush administration has extended the crony capitalism it pursued in Iraq by offering no-contract bids at home to the same corporate giants of industry: Halliburton,

Bechtel, and Ashbritt, among others. As Mike Davis observes:

> The paramount beneficiaries of Katrina relief aid have been the giant engineering firms KBR (a Halliburton subsidiary) and the Shaw Group, which enjoy the services of lobbyist Joe Allbaugh (a former FEMA director and Bush's 2000 campaign manager). FEMA and the Army Corps of Engineers, while unable to explain to Governor Blanco last fall exactly how they were spending money in Louisiana, have tolerated levels of profiteering that would raise eyebrows even on the war-torn Euphrates. (Some of this largesse, of course, is guaranteed to be recycled as GOP campaign contributions.) FEMA, for example, has paid the Shaw Group $175 per square (100 square feet) to install tarps on the storm-damaged roofs in New Orleans. Yet the actual installers earn as little as $2 per square, and the tarps are provided by FEMA.... Every level of the contracting food chain, in other words, is grotesquely overfed except the bottom rung, where the actual work is carried out. While the Friends of Bush mine gold from the wreckage of New Orleans, many disappointed recovery workers–often Mexican or Salvadorian immigrants camped out in city parks and derelict shopping centers–can barely make ends meet.[142]

In fact, Katrina, for many Republicans, has delivered the Gulf Coast as a laboratory for experimenting with and enacting full-scale privatization and market-based reforms. The tireless champions of market fundamentalism view the recovery effort as an opportunity to push for school choice, vouchers for health care, corporate tax abatements, deregulation—in short, for "turning the entire region into a massive enterprise zone."[143] President Bush's pledge "to get the work done" by mounting "one of the largest reconstruction efforts the world has ever seen"[144] not only has turned into a profit-bearing handout for his corporate cronies but also has energized the white power elite to reconfigure New Orleans in the mode of Disney World—that is, as a city largely purged of its former black and brown inhabitants. Moreover, faith-based groups are once again being called upon by the Bush administration to do the work of government, in spite of the all-too-visible disdain for public values embodied by many of Bush's religious allies. Instead of creating the conditions to rethink the obligations of government to its citizens, the Bush administration has turned the Katrina disaster into a potential fantasy land for greed, profiteering, and political favoritism as "[h]undreds of companies are rushing for the Gold."[145] While the cost of rebuilding the Gulf Coast has been estimated at $200 billion, the right-wing market fundamentalists in Congress, encouraged by this unanticipated opportunity, have already pointed to the huge expense as a rationale for instituting thus far over $40 billion worth of cutbacks in programs such as Medicaid, student loans, food stamps, and other programs that serve the poor, vulnerable, and youth in American society.[146] As the "hidden hand of free-market politics and the corporate elite" is coupled with the "iron fist of military force,"[147] New Orleans will come to model the new ethos of biopolitics and disposability. Before Hurricane Katrina, New Orleans was 70 percent black, but because many of the largest black neighborhoods were lost in the flood, the percentage is now much lower, with as many as 80 percent of the city's black residents still dispersed throughout the country. Race has played a significant role in the recovery efforts, with some people in the business community and the elite classes calling for a smaller city—a not-too-subtle way of arguing for a whiter city. Others in the community are making race a "subtext for just about every contentious decision the city faces: where to put FEMA trailers; which neighborhoods to rebuild; how the troubled school system should be reorganized."[148] Dorothy Stukes, a spokeswoman for the ACORN Katrina Survivors Association, argues that the New Orleans Rebuilding Commission's plan for issuing building permits puts forth a "standard for a 'viable'" African-American neighbourhood "that has nothing to do with ecology or engineering. It has everything to do with race and wealth."[149] Commenting on the Bush administration's lack of progress in producing the funds and legislation needed to rebuild the homes of minorities of class and color, Representative Barney Frank (D-Mass.) called such neglect "a policy of ethnic cleansing by inaction."[150] It is difficult under the circumstances not to view the rebuilding of New Orleans as a logic and strategy inextricably tied to a politics of disposability, the consequence of which will mean that the city will be racially cleansed, and the poisonous legacy of racial exclusion will appear under the guise of recovery and urban reform, performed under the watchful eye of the armed forces and the local police.[151] David Theo Goldberg, in light of the current rebuilding efforts, writes presciently about how the politics of disposability will play out in the city's recovery.

> The rebuilding of New Orleans will be instructive too. A city with no residents for the foreseeable future, it will be turned into a Disneyland for the oil industry where the racial poor will

not be welcomed back (after all, they have been disbursed and dispersed to larger more heterogeneous cities where their presence ultimately will become less noticed). The working class will service the oil rich and worry free. The pollution will be rendered invisible in landfills and waterways once again to afflict the most vulnerable. A new sports stadium supporting privately owned sports teams valued at hundreds of millions of dollars each will be sponsored by oil revenue. Mardi Gras will be turned from the conviviality of an organic urban celebration to the plasticity of tourist fanfare. New Orleans spirit reduced to the cloned parades of Mickeys and Minnies.[152]

A rebuilt New Orleans will attract very few of the minorities of class and color who left the city, and if it does they will be living in trailers, housing projects, and run-down hotel rooms serving the needs of the rich who will either live in or visit this new Disneyfied resort site.[153] The militarization of New Orleans is also instructive in that it suggests a link between Iraq and New Orleans, both of which point to war as a fundamental organizing principle of politics and to militarism as the most important mechanism for holding society together.[154] In both Iraq and New Orleans, humanistic values have given way to militaristic values as life is cheapened, the reality of death is diminished, and civil society increasingly "organizes itself for the production of violence."[155] War now has no boundaries and is used as a metaphor to define and criminalize those populations rendered as racialized others—whether they are blacks, Latinos, immigrants, Muslims, or Arabs. Not only is a war increasingly waged against the racialized poor at home and abroad, but the attack on the welfare state, the growing redundancy and dis-

posability of large segments of those marginalized by
class and race, and the increasing criminalization of
social problems and reliance on the police and military
to solve them point to an emerging biopolitics in the
United States that bears the fingerprints of a growing
authoritarianism.

The politics of disaster that affected Louisiana,
Alabama, and Mississippi is about more than government incompetence, militarization, socioeco-
nomic polarization, rampant racism, environmental
disaster, and political scandal; it's about what these
elements add up to together. It is primarily about a
new kind of biopolitics, one that is divested of democratic principles, practices, and values and scornful
of the social contract. It is a biopolitics driven by the
waste machine of what Zygmunt Bauman defines as
"liquid modernity."[156] Global neoliberalism and its
victims now occupy a space shaped by authoritarian
politics, the terrors inflicted by a police state, and a
logic of disposability that removes them from government social provisions and from the discourse and
privileges of citizenship. Treated as redundant, people
marginalized by class and race are considered either
dangerous or worthless, left to fight off society's misfortunes alone, with no one but themselves to rely on.
They are the products of an economic Darwinism that
now operates unabashedly in public view, producing
entire populations that pass quickly into human waste
machines so as to be neither a drain on the privileged
classes nor a burden on public consciousness. Under
such circumstances, disposable populations are an
inevitable and just corollary of a biopolitics that takes
pride in the construction of a neoliberal order. Victims
of destroyed levees, they live amidst devastated cities,
and in broken schools. Legions of the dispossessed
occupy those disaster zones hidden away from and

locked out of gated communities and heavily guarded suburban malls. When their presence and behavior are noticed, they are demonized; and the struggles they face on a daily level are defined as issues of concern only for those agencies that prosecute criminal activities.

Conclusion

Anyone who cannot cope with life while he is alive needs one hand to ward off a little of his despair over his fate.... [B]ut with his other hand he can jot down what he sees among the ruins, for he sees different and more things than the others; after all, he is dead in his own lifetime and the real survivor.

—*Franz Kafka*[157]

Katrina reveals that we are living in dark times. The shadow of authoritarianism remains after the storm clouds and hurricane winds have passed, offering a glimpse of its wreckage and terror. Under the Orwellian politics of Big Brother and the economic logic of disposability, both dissent and those deemed redundant, economically and politically, are removed from the discourse, values, and space of a substantive democracy. As the state becomes more militarized, not only do civil liberties begin to disappear but so do human beings. The Bush government brazenly defends spying on Americans without a warrant and implements the reprehensible practice of extraordinary rendition as people such as Canadian citizen Maher Arar are kidnapped by American authorities and sent to foreign countries such as Syria to be tortured.[158] But dissenters and alleged terrorists are not the only ones being punished or "disappeared" in this new world order. Those who are poor minorities of color and class, unable to contribute to the prevailing consumerist ethic, vanish, too, into the sinkhole of poverty in desolate and abandoned enclaves of decaying cities, neighborhoods, and rural spaces, or in America's ever-expanding prison empire. War has become the medium for conducting politics at home and abroad, and its guiding principles can be seen in a text written for Republican Party activists by ultra-right-winger and "latter-day Carl Schmitt," David Horowitz, who set the tone for the 2000 Republican presidential campaign. Horowitz's book, *The Art of War and Other Political Pursuits,* provided an exemplary discourse for the new biopolitical agenda of the Bush administration. The slogan "politics is war conducted by other means" not only disbanded democratic notions of debate and argument, not to mention accountability, from both the realm of politics and the public sphere, but also called for "destroying the enemy's fighting ability."[159] This is a biopolitics that operates within the duelling discourses of good and evil, views dissent as treason, and incorporates exclusion and moral indifference as a productive strategy of political life itself. Within this discursive strategy, the rhetoric of war and evil "exacerbates the deadly politics of power by operating under a rhetorical spell of sacred duties and diabolical enemies ... [and] transforms the act of killing ... and/or destroying life-sustaining infrastructures into a necessary and legitimate consequence of exercising righteous force over a demonic antagonist."[160] Biopolitics in this context is linked to the securing of borders to prevent the influx of immigrants, the production of human waste removal mechanisms to dispose of those populations considered dangerous or redundant, and the acquisition of profit-heavy portfolios. Under the

Bush regime, biopolitics registers a new and brutal racism as part of the emergence of a new and brutal authoritarianism.

The biopolitical commitments of the Bush regime must be challenged and removed if there is any chance for democracy to survive in the United States. Progressives appear to be in a conceptual crisis in terms of how both to define politics and to provide the political and educational conditions to enable people to challenge the most basic institutions, values, ideologies, and pedagogical practices that drive the new authoritarianism. Against the neoliberal assumption that markets and democracy are the same, a spirited challenge to this oxymoron has to be waged at all levels of struggle. Democracy has to be reclaimed and its relationship to the principles of liberty, equality, and freedom reaffirmed and struggled over as part of a renewed commitment for social and economic justice, on the one hand, and for global democracy, on the other. But the fight over democracy is not merely about the fight for noble ideals and ideas; it is also a fight over power, public space, the pedagogical conditions necessary for critical citizenship, and the struggle for those public institutions that articulate and defend the welfare state and the social contract along with the economic, cultural, and political conditions necessary for all people to become engaged individual and social agents.

Any viable attempt to challenge the biopolitical project that now shapes American life and culture must be organized through a multifaceted third party or, as Stanley Aronowitz argues, a radical party. In this case, a group must be willing to provide the tools for public understanding by organizing intellectuals, artists, workers, and others who can dedicate themselves to theorizing, studying, and engaging in local and larger struggles. Aronowitz further argues that a new party must not only address the concerns of the working and middle classes but must also join with "rank-and-file activists of trade unions, women's organizations, environmental and ecology movements, various factions of the freedom movements for Blacks, Latinos, Asians, and other oppressed peoples, and the anti-war and global justice movements" to expose the illusion of democracy in the United States.[161] Even then, it must do more than unearth the powerful anti-democratic forces that now govern American economics, politics, education, media, and culture; it must also deepen the possibility of individual and collective struggles by fighting for the rebuilding of civil society and the creation of a vast network of democratic public spheres such as schools and the alternative media in order to develop new models of individual and social agency that can expand the reality of democratic public life. Democratically minded citizens and social movements must return to the crucial issue of how race, class, power, and inequality in America contribute to the suffering and hardships experienced daily by the poor, people of color, and working- and middle-class people. The fight for equality offers new challenges in the process of constructing a politics that directly addresses poverty, class domination, and a resurgent racism. Such a politics would take seriously what it means to struggle pedagogically and politically over both the ideas and the material relations of power as they affect diverse individuals and groups at the level of daily life. Such struggles would combine a democratically energized cultural politics of resistance and hope with a politics aimed at offering a living wage and a guaranteed standard of living—one that provides housing, health care, and a decent education to all residents of the United

States. This is a call for a diverse radical party that prioritizes democracy as a global task, views hope as a precondition for political engagement, gives primacy to making the political more pedagogical, and understands the importance of the totality of the struggle as it informs and articulates within and across a wide range of sites and sectors of everyday life—domestically and globally.

Biopolitics is not just about the reduction of selected elements of the population to the necessities of bare life or worse; it is also potentially about enhancing life by linking hope and a new vision to the struggle for reclaiming the social, providing a language capable of translating individual issues into public consid- erations, and recognizing that in the age of the new media the terrain of culture is one of the most impor- tant pedagogical spheres through which to challenge the most basic precepts of the new authoritarianism. Politics has to take a detour through multiple webs of knowledge, affective investments, and values that circulate throughout the larger culture. It is within these sites, with their diverse public pedagogies, that subjects are formed, identifications made, actions contemplated, and social relations put into play. The waste machine of modernity, as Bauman points out, must be challenged within a new understanding of environmental justice, human rights, and democratic politics. Negative globalization, with its attachment to the mutually enforcing modalities of militarism and racial segregation, must be exposed and dismantled. And this demands new forms of resistance that are both more global and differentiated. But if these struggles are going to emerge, especially in the United States, then we need a politics and pedagogy of hope, one that takes seriously Hannah Arendt's call to use the public realm to throw light on the "dark times" that threaten to extinguish the very idea of democracy. Such an ambitious project suggests new ways of thinking about culture as complex and contested sites of struggle over concrete experience, the relationships of cultural politics to democratic life and learning to social change, and modes of literacy that refuse the barbarism of market fundamentalism and racial exclusion. In turn, these new ways of thinking mean applying Theodor Adorno's observation that "[t]hinking is not the intellectual reproduction of what already exists.... As long as it doesn't break off, thinking has a secure hold on possibility. Its insatiable aspect, its aversion to being quickly and easily satisfied, refuses the foolish wisdom of resignation.... Open thinking points beyond itself."[162] And it is this "beyond itself" that indicates the need for new discursive strategies, politics, and vision that address those shared beliefs and practices aimed at creating more inclusive democracies on a global scale. Such shared beliefs must emerge out of a project that rejects a biopolitics of disposability that embraces bigotry while criminalizing difference and enshrines common sense over critical reason. Against the tyranny of market fundamentalism, religious dogmatism, unchecked militarism, and ideological claims to certainty, an oppositional biopolitics must enlist education as a crucial force in the struggle over democratic identities, spaces, and ideals.

The new authoritarianism dominates popular culture, the media, and the culture industry. All of these spheres must be understood not only through the discourse of political economy but also as crucial forms of public pedagogy that are integral to producing the meanings, values, affective investments, and ideologies that tie people to the logic of racism, to the escalating militarism of the national security state, and to their own indifference to the obligations of public responsibility. What modes of persuasion and bonds of empathy work within the schools and the larger culture to align people with the growing vulgar fundamentalisms so central to the Bush regime that revel in religious dogmatism, an egregious nationalism, an exploitative market-based ideology, and the exclusionary fault lines of race and class? Instead of condemning the general public as politically illiterate, bigoted, racist, socially indifferent, or powerless, it is more useful to understand how the public is educated to accept the false notion that a ruthless pursuit of private interests and satisfaction of individual needs constitute the only conditions of citizenship. The larger culture encourages people to support policies and ideologies that dismantle the very public spheres that are crucial to their own development as citizens and social agents, to allow their country to lie about the reasons for going to war while sitting back silently when American soldiers and Iraqi citizens are needlessly killed, to passively accept being spied on illegally by the government, and to tolerate right-wing attempts to undermine the politics of hope. What might it mean to instead educate people to temper what they see, read, hear, and experience through a politics of possibility that affirms democratic solidarity, planetary humanism, and multicultural global democracy? What might it mean to link education not merely to modes of self-discovery, self-criticism, and social criticism but also to social responsibility and collective action, particularly in the service of expanding and deepening the "democratic, secular, and open character"[163] of contemporary society?

Central to an oppositional biopolitics is the recognition that abiding powerlessness atrophies the public imagination and leads to political paralysis. Consequently, its policies avidly attack critical education at all levels of cultural production in an all-out effort to undermine critical thought, imagination, and substantive agency. To significantly confront the force of a biopolitics in the service of the new authoritarianism, intellectuals, artists, and others in various cultural sites—from schools to higher education to the media—will have to rethink what it means to secure the conditions for critical education both within and outside of the schools. In the context of formal schooling, this means fighting against the corporatization, commercialism, and privatization of public schools. The right wing has waged a fierce struggle to privatize public education, turn it over to the forces of standardization and test-taking, or force it to fail through economic disinvestment so that it can then be privatized. The aim here is to remove such schools from their traditional role as democratic public spheres—banishing from them any notion of learning connected to critical thinking, engaged citizenship, expanded notions of cultural and political literacy, and critical pedagogy. If public values are to be made visible, schools must be defended along with life-long education, not only for the acquisition of skills but also for the capacities they impart that enable students and others to exercise the agency and courage necessary both to hold power accountable and to intervene in the world in order to expand the range of knowledge, democratic values, choices, and social possibilities open to them. In short, instead of removing schooling from the realm of politics and power, progressives and other cultural workers need to assert and defend its meaning and purpose in a democratic society. Higher education has to be defended in the same terms. Increasingly influenced by a troika of power consisting of corporate interests, the national security state, and right-wing ideologues who want to strip higher education of its critical functions, American universities must be defended as a crucial site for the development of critical ideas, inclusive social relations, and democratic values.

Against the biopolitics of racial exclusion, the university should be a principal site where dialogue, negotiation, mutual understanding, and respect provide the knowledge and experience for students to develop a shared space for affirming differences while simultaneously learning those shared values necessary for an inclusive democratic society. Similarly, both public and higher education must address with new courage the history of American slavery, the enduring legacy of racism in the United States, and its interface with both political nationalism and the enduring market and religious fundamentalisms at work in contemporary society. Workers, citizens, parents, artists, and others must reject the substitution of training for critical education, the hijacking of critical pedagogy by therapeutic models of learning, and the divestiture of the language of politics, ethics, and power from modes of learning. Higher education must infuse the humanities with a renewed and extended interest in understanding the contributions of people of color both in the United States and abroad, and how such contributions in politics, philosophy, arts, music, film, literature, nonfiction writing, science, and other realms have impacted American culture and life.[164] Similarly, racism must not be reduced to a private matter, a case of individual prejudice removed from the dictates of state violence and the broader realm of politics, and left to matters of "taste, preference, and ultimately, of consumer, or lifestyle choice."[165] What must be instituted and fought for in higher education is a critical and anti-racist pedagogy that unsettles, stirs up human consciousness, "breeds dissatisfaction with the level of both freedom and democracy achieved thus far," and inextricably connects the fates of freedom, democracy, and critical education.[166]

Hannah Arendt once argued that "the public realm has lost the power of illumination," and one result is that more and more people "have retreated from the world and their obligations within it."[167] The public realm is not merely a space where the political, social, economic, and cultural interconnect; it is also the preeminent space of public pedagogy—that is, a space where subjectivities are shaped, public commitments are formed, and choices are made. As sites of cultural politics and public pedagogy, public spheres offer a unique opportunity for critically engaged citizens, young people, academics, teachers, and various intellectuals to engage in pedagogical struggles that provide the conditions for social empowerment and "the rebuilding of the now increasingly deserted public space where men and women may engage in continuous translation between the individual and the common, the private and the communal interests, rights and duties."[168] Such struggles can be waged through the new media, films, publications, radio interviews, and a range of other forms of cultural production. It is especially crucial, as Mark Poster has argued, that academics and cultural theorists take on the challenge of understanding how the new media technologies construct subjects differently with multiple forms of literacy that engage a range of intellectual capacities.[169] The new technologies of technoculture are powerful pedagogical tools that need to be used in the struggle against both dominant media and the hegemonic ideologies they produce, circulate, and legitimate.

Making pedagogy and education central to the political tasks of reclaiming public space, rekindling the importance of public connectedness, and infusing civic life with the importance of a democratic worldly vision are at the heart of opposing the new authoritarianism. Hannah Arendt recognized that any viable democratic politics must address the totality of public life, refusing to withdraw from such a challenge in the face of totalitarian violence that legitimates itself through appeals to safety, fear, and the threat of terrorism. She writes: "Terror becomes total when it becomes independent of all opposition; it rules supreme when nobody any longer stands in its way. If lawfulness is the essence of non-tyrannical government and lawlessness is the essence of tyranny, then terror is the essence of totalitarian domination."[170] The promise of a better world cannot be found in modes of authority that lack a vision of social justice, renounce the promise of democracy, and reject the dream of a better future, offering instead of dreams the pale assurance of protection from the nightmare of an all-embracing terrorism. Against this stripped-down legitimation of authority is the promise of public spheres that in their diverse forms, sites, and content offer pedagogical and political possibilities for strengthening the social bonds of democracy, new spaces from which to cultivate the capacities for critical modes of individual and social agency, and crucial opportunities to form alliances to collectively struggle for an oppositional biopolitics that expands the scope of vision, the operations of democracy, and the range of democratic institutions—that is, a biopolitics that fights against the terrors of totalitarianism. Such spheres are about more than legal rights guaranteeing freedom of speech; they are also sites that demand a certain kind of citizen informed by particular forms of education, a citizen whose education provides the essential conditions for democratic public spheres to flourish. Cornelius

Castoriadis, the great philosopher of democracy, argues that if public space is to be experienced not as a private affair but as a vibrant sphere in which people experience and learn how to participate in and shape public life, it must be shaped through an education that provides the decisive traits of courage, responsibility, and respect, all of which connect the fate of each individual to the fate of others, the planet, and global democracy.[171] To confront the biopolitics of disposability, of which the political disaster of Katrina offers an exemplary case, we need to recognize the dark times in which we live and offer up a vision of hope that creates the conditions for multiple collective and global struggles that refuse to use politics as an act of war and markets as the measure of democracy. Making human beings superfluous is the essence of totalitarianism, and democracy is the antidote in urgent need of being reclaimed. Katrina should keep the hope of such a struggle alive for quite some time because for many of us the images of those floating bodies serve as a desperate reminder of what it means when justice, as the lifeblood of democracy, becomes cold and indifferent in the face of death.

As I have pointed out in this chapter, Katrina is symptomatic of a much larger crisis in the United States—a crisis that threatens the very nature of individual freedom and democracy. This is a crisis that extends far beyond matters of leadership and governance; it is a crisis at the very heart of democratic politics and social justice. In the next chapter, I want to situate the events surrounding Hurricane Katrina within such a crisis by analyzing the broader set of anti-democratic forces that made the social disaster underlying Katrina possible. And, in the process of doing so, I want to examine these anti-democratic tendencies as part of an emerging authoritarianism in the

United States. I also want to address some important elements of an oppositional biopolitics.

The United States is at war at home and abroad, and in both cases human rights, civil liberties, economic justice, and the promise of democracy are being shredded. War, fear, and violence have become the primary forces forging a dirty democracy at home and an imperialist adventure abroad. Empire abroad is matched by a growing authoritarianism on the domestic front. Katrina represents not simply the failing of government responsibility but the emergence of a new kind of biopolitical commitment in which government is being refashioned according to the interests of an overzealous market-based fundamentalism, an all-embracing militarism, a religious extremism, and right-wing mullahs waging an assault on critical thought and dissent. Central to all of these fundamentalisms is a hatred of genuine democracy, a thirst for political conformity, a quest for a transnational empire, and the removal of the human costs of capital from ethical and political constraints. Just as most Iraqis are locked out of the possibility of governing their own society, most Americans have little to say about influencing the major forces shaping their lives. Hope and critical thought have little value in the current historical moment as insecurity, fear, and terrorism provide the dominant narratives that shape American life. The shadow of authoritarianism is conditioned less by dreams than by nightmares. Disposable populations are now on the receiving end of the discourses of redundancy, moral absolutes, and certainty. The stripped-down language of outsourcing, flexibility, and contract labor cleanses the market of those elements of the population who become superfluous as workers. Religious fundamentalists invoke a notion of radical evil "making human beings superfluous as human beings."[172] Ideological fundamentalists wage a war against critical thought so as to make it difficult for human beings either to reject rigid principles and black-and-white dichotomies or to hold government and corporate power accountable. Immigrants and poor people of color are now coded as refugees, criminals, and a threat to the American way of life and Western civilization. Government appeals to evil and the war on terrorism now justify, if not mimic, the very authoritarian practices they claim to be fighting. The Bush government along with dominant public spheres ranging from the media to higher education increasingly appear to be stifling understanding and interpretation rather than inviting students, youth, adults, educators, and others to think, debate, confront important social issues, and resist moral certainties and absolutes. The stifling and dangerous anti-democratic tendencies that transformed a natural disaster into a human and social tragedy are still at work in American society, prompting a collapse of the public and leaving no place for individual and social agency that is responsive to the deepest social conflicts and problems of our time. In order for a substantive and inclusive notion of democracy to be reclaimed, it is crucial to identify through a language of understanding, critique, and possibility the most serious threats to democracy along with the conditions that make individual and collective resistance to such threats possible. Katrina has exposed a new biopolitics in which entire populations have become disposable; it has also revealed the necessity to rethink what it means to fight for democracy in a complex, global world. This suggests addressing those elements of an oppositional biopolitics that situate the struggle for global democracy in the transnational as the new terrain upon which to imagine concrete antidotes to the legacies of colonialism, racism, and authoritarianism along with the very real class, race, and gender inequalities that mark contemporary places and contexts of suffering, struggle, and resistance. It is to these issues in the next chapter that I now turn.

◇

2

Dirty Democracy and State Authoritarianism

Dirty Democracy in America

Revelations in the *New York Times* about the Bush administration's decision to allow the National Security Agency to spy on Americans without first obtaining warrants, the disclosure by the *Washington Post* of a network of covert prisons known as "black sites" established by the Central Intelligence Agency (CIA) in eight countries, the rampant corruption involving some of the most powerful politicians in the Bush administration, the Bush administration's political and moral laxity in the face of the Katrina tragedy, and the ongoing stories about widespread abuse and torture in Iraq and Afghanistan are just some of the elements in the popular press that point to a growing authoritarianism in American life. The government, as many notable and courageous critics ranging from Seymour M. Hersh to Gore Vidal and Robert Kennedy Jr. have pointed out, is now in the hands of extremists who have shredded civil liberties, lied to the American public to legitimize sending young American troops to Iraq, and alienated most of the international community with a blatant exercise of arrogant power.

These right-wing extremists have also tarnished the highest offices of government with unsavory corporate alliances, used political power unabashedly to pursue legislative policies that favor the rich and punish the poor, and disabled those public spheres not governed by the logic of the market. Sidney Blumenthal, a former senior adviser to President Clinton and no radical, has argued that the Bush administration has created a government that is tantamount to "a national security state of torture, ghost detainees, secret prisons, renditions and domestic eavesdropping."[1] The consequences of the new U.S. imperium for global democracy are no less dramatic.

In the United States, a silent war is being waged against poor young people and people of color who are being either warehoused in substandard schools or incarcerated at alarming rates. But these are not the only targets. Universities are accused of being soft on terrorism and un-American in their critiques of the Bush administration; homophobia has become the poster-ideology of the Republican Party; the Republican Congress is waging a frontal assault on undocumented immigrants; and a full-fledged assault on women's reproductive rights is being championed by Bush's evangelical supporters—most evident in Bush's recent Supreme Court appointments. While the legal rights and support services of people of color, the poor, youth, the middle class, the elderly, gays, and women are being attacked, the current administration is supporting a campaign to collapse the boundaries between church and state to the extent that even liberal critics such as Frank Rich believe that the United States is on the verge of becoming a fundamentalist theocracy.[2]

As war becomes the foundation for an empire-driven foreign policy in the United States, real and symbolic violence combine with a number of anti-democratic tendencies to make the world more dangerous and the promise of global democracy difficult to imagine in the current historical moment. Ultranationalistic imagery of empire disseminated by a largely right-wing media, now an echo chamber for the Bush administration, has made militaristic symbols widespread throughout American culture, reasserting racial hierarchies associated with earlier forms of colonialism. The language of patriotic correctness and religious fanaticism is beginning to replace the language of social justice and equality, bespeaking the enduring attraction if not "rehabilitation of fascist ideas and principles."[3] Indeed, war and warriors have become the most endearing models of national greatness. As the United States invokes jingoistic and anti-democratic policies through a notion of sovereignty legitimized as a never-ending war on terrorism, global democracy is now compromised. Rejecting any form of internationalism at odds with its own global interests, the United States is currently refashioning a notion of sovereignty defined through a biopolitics in which "daily life and the functioning of power has been permeated with the threat and violence of warfare."[4] Human beings are no longer protected by domestic and international law, and state violence has become the defining feature of the imperial rogue state. As instruments of unchecked biopower, law and violence have become indistinguishable, and sovereignty is reduced to waging a war on terrorism that mimics the very terror it claims to be fighting. Within this notion of sovereignty, state violence is organized around the mutually determining forces of security and terrorism that increasingly "form a single deadly system, in which they justify and legitimate each others' actions."[5] Whereas the Clinton administration situated its key positions in the Treasury Department, the Bush administration relies on its defense experts—Cheney, Rumsfeld, and Rice—to develop its international policy. Within this view of sovereignty and power, Bush and his cohorts show they understand well the new imperialist role of the United States, especially "the connection between internal and external order. They intuitively accepted [Hannah] Arendt's view that empire abroad entails tyranny at home, but state it differently. Military activity abroad requires military-like discipline at home."[6]

While it would be ludicrous to suggest that the United States either represents a mirror image of fascist ideology or mimics the systemic racialized terror of Nazi Germany, it is not unreasonable, as Hannah Arendt urged in *The Origins of Totalitarianism*, to learn to recognize how various elements of fascism crystallize in distinct historical periods into new forms of authoritarianism. Such anti-democratic elements combine in often unpredictable ways, and I believe they can be found currently in many of the political practices, values, and policies that characterize U.S. sovereignty under the Bush administration. Unchecked power at the top of the political hierarchy is increasingly matched by an aggressive attack on dissent throughout the body politic and fuels both a war abroad and a war at home. The economic and militaristic powers of global capital—spearheaded by U.S. corporations and political interests—appear uncurbed by traditional forms of national and international sovereignty, the implications of which are captured in David Harvey's serviceable phrase "accumulation by dispossession."[7] Entire populations are now seen as disposable, marking a dangerous moment for the promise of a global democracy.[8] The discourse of liberty, equality, and freedom that emerged with modernity seems to have lost even its residual value as the central project of democracy. State sovereignty is no longer organized around the struggle for life but now entails an insatiable quest for the accumulation of capital, leading to what Achille Mbembe calls "necropolitics" or the destruction of human bodies.[9] War, violence, and death have become the principal elements shaping the biopolitics of the new authoritarianism that is emerging in the United States and increasingly extending its reach into broader global spheres, from Iraq to a vast array of military outposts and prisons around the world.

Market Fundamentalism and the Ethos of Privatize or Perish

As the state of emergency, in Giorgio Agamben's aptly chosen words, becomes the rule rather than the exception, a number of powerful anti-democratic tendencies threaten the prospects for both American and global democracy.[10] The first is a market fundamentalism that not only trivializes democratic values and public concerns but also enshrines a rabid individualism, an all-embracing quest for profits, and a social Darwinism in which misfortune is seen as weakness—the current sum total being the Hobbesian rule of a "war of all against all" that replaces any vestige of shared responsibilities or compassion for others. The totalizing belief that the market should be unregulated is equally matched by the belief "that every domain of human life should be open to the forces of the marketplace."[11] The values of the market and the ruthless workings of finance capital become the template for organizing the rest of society. Everybody is now a customer or client, and every relationship is ultimately judged in bottom-line, cost-effective terms as the neoliberal mantra "privatize or perish" is repeated over and over again. Responsible citizens are replaced by an assemblage of entrepreneurial subjects, each tempered in the virtue of self-reliance and forced to face the increasingly difficult challenges of the social order alone. Instead of society with its expanse of civil institutions and public goods, neoliberalism recognizes only individuals, families, and firms as worthy of any kind of agency or value. Freedom, no longer about securing equality, social justice, or the public welfare, is now about unhampered trade in goods, financial capital, and commodities. As the logic of capital trumps democratic sovereignty, low-intensity warfare at home chips away at democratic freedoms, and high-intensity warfare abroad delivers democracy with bombs, tanks, and chemical warfare.

The global cost of these neoliberal commitments is massive human suffering and death, delivered not only in the form of bombs and the barbaric practices of occupying armies but also in structural adjustment policies in which the drive for land, resources, profits, and goods is implemented by global financial institutions such as the World Bank and the International Monetary Fund. Global lawlessness and armed violence accompany the imperative of free trade, the virtues of a market without boundaries, and the promise of a Western-style democracy imposed through military solutions, ushering in the age of rogue sovereignty on a global scale. Under such conditions, human suffering and hardship reach unprecedented levels of intensity. In a rare moment of truth, Thomas Friedman, the famous columnist for the *New York Times*, precisely argued for the use of U.S. power—including military force—to support this anti-democratic world order, claiming that "[t]he hidden hand of the market will never work without the hidden fist. . . . And the hidden fist that keeps the world safe for Silicon Valley's technologies to flourish is called the US Army, Air Force,

Navy and Marine Corps."[12] As Mark Rupert points out, "In Friedman's twisted world, if people are to realize their deepest aspirations—the longing for a better life which comes from their very souls—they must stare down the barrel of Uncle Sam's gun."[13]

Under market fundamentalism, the market free of regulation and the self-interested striving of individuals become the cornerstones of both freedom and democracy. As Lawrence Grossberg points out, "The free market in neoliberalism is fundamentally an argument against politics, or at least against a politics that attempts to govern society in social rather than economic terms."[14] As neoliberals in the Bush administration implement policies at home to reduce taxation and regulation while spending billions on wars abroad, they slash funds that benefit the sick, the elderly, the poor, and young people. But public resources are diverted not only from crucial domestic problems ranging from poverty and unemployment to hunger; they are also diverted from addressing the fate of some 45 million children in "the world's poor countries [who] will die needlessly over the next decade," as reported by the British-based group Oxfam.[15] The U.S. commitment to market fundamentalism elevates profits over human needs and consequently offers few displays of compassion, aid, or relief for millions of poor and abandoned children in the world who do not have adequate shelter, who are severely hungry, who have no access to health care or safe water, and who succumb needlessly to the ravages of AIDS and other diseases.[16] For instance, as Jim Lobe points out, "U.S. foreign aid in 2003 ranked dead-last among all wealthy nations. In fact, its entire development aid spending in 2003 came to only ten percent of what it spent on the Iraq war that year. U.S. development assistance comes to less than one-fortieth of its annual defense budget."[17] Carol Bellamy, the executive director of UNICEF, outlines the consequences of the broken promises to children by advanced capitalist countries such as the United States. She writes:

Today more than one billion children are suffering extreme deprivations from poverty, war, and HIV/AIDS. The specifics are staggering: 640 million children without adequate shelter, 400 million children without access to safe water, and 270 million children without access to basic health services. AIDS has orphaned 15 million children. During the 1990s alone, war forced 20 million children to leave their homes.[18]

With the death of Keynesianism and the rise of a "free market" unchecked by government intervention, regulation, and control, the compulsion to accumulate capital now overrides social provisions for the poor, elderly, and youth. Individual responsibility has replaced investing in the common good or taking seriously the imperatives of the social contract that informed the earlier policies of the New Deal and President Lyndon Johnson's Great Society programs of the 1960s. Advocates of neoliberalism wage a war against the gains of the welfare state, renounce its commitment to collective provision of public goods, and ruthlessly urge the urban poor, homeless, elderly, and disabled to rely on their own initiative. As the government is hollowed out, privatization schemes infect all aspects of society. As the state gives up its role as the guardian of the public interest and public goods, reactionary politics takes the place of democratic governance. "The hijacking of public policy by private interests," Paul Krugman observes, parallels "the downward spiral in governance."[19] And one consequence is a growing gap between the rich and the poor and the downward spiral of millions of Americans into poverty and despair. The haunting images of dead bodies floating in the flooded streets of New Orleans following Hurricane Katrina, along with thousands of African-Americans stranded in streets, abandoned in the Louisiana Superdome, and waiting to be rescued for days on the roofs of flooded houses serve as just one register of the despairing racism, inequality, and poverty in America. As I mentioned in Chapter 1, the stark realities of race and class divisions along with the widening reach of poverty, racism, and the abuse of human rights are visible in an array of troubling statistics. For instance, the rate of child poverty rose in 2004 to 17.6 percent, boosting the number of poor children to 13 million. For African-Americans the poverty rate was twice the national rate with 24.4 percent of blacks living below the poverty line. Moreover, children are a disproportionate share of the poor in the United States. Although they are 26 percent of the total population, they constitute 39 percent of the poor. Over 45 million people are uninsured in the United States, and the number has increased by 6 million since 2000, the year George W. Bush was appointed to the presidency.[20] Put into a more global context, it gets even worse:

> According to statistics from the Bread for the World Institute, 3.5 percent of U.S. households experience hunger (9.6 million people, including 3 million children.).... UNICEF states that although the U.S. is still the wealthiest country on Earth, with income levels higher than any other country, it also has one of the highest incidences of child poverty among the rich, industrialized nations.

Denmark and Finland have child-poverty levels of less than 3 percent, and are closely followed by Norway and Sweden, thanks to higher levels of social spending.[21]

With the rise of market fundamentalism, economics is accorded more respect than human needs, human rights, and democratic values; the citizen has been reduced to a consumer—the buying and selling of goods are all that seem to matter. Even children are now targeted as a constituency from which to make money, as they are reduced to commodities, sexualized in endless advertisements, and shamelessly treated as a market for huge profits. Market fundamentalism not only makes time a burden for those without health insurance, child care, a decent job, and adequate social services; it also commercializes and privatizes public space, undermining both the idea of citizenship and those very spaces and spheres (schools, media, labor unions, etc.) needed to make it a vigorous and engaged force for a substantive democracy.

Anti-democratic tendencies gain power as forces such as labor unions, which "once constrained corporate economic and political power,"[22] are dissolved. As the United States wages a relentless attack on union membership at home, now totalling a mere 7.9 percent of the labor force in the private sector, it reinforces the neoliberal backlash against organized labor throughout the globe (though with increasing resistance in Latin America). At the same time, the rabid neoliberalism of the Bush administration fuels global policies that threaten the environment, especially in light of the Bush government's refusal to sign the Kyoto Protocol, designed to control greenhouse gas emissions and reduce global warming. In addition, the United States was the only nation to oppose the International Plan for Cleaner Energy put forth by the Group of Eight (G-8) in 2001. Once again, the authoritarianism of the Bush government represents a poisonous form of biopolitics in which unnecessary deaths appear utterly reasonable, especially if the "disposable populations" interfere with the system of accumulation under globalized monopoly capitalism. Waste, growing inequality, global warming, the rise in world sea levels, the decline of ecosystems on earth, and the extinction of many plant and animal species appear to the Bush administration to be a small price to pay for promoting the logic and reaping the rewards of market fundamentalism. And the consequences impact not just the United States but the entire globe, especially those nations that are defenseless to protect themselves from the toxins, waste, environmental damage, and economic looting affecting their villages, cities, and neighborhoods. Under such circumstances, hope is foreclosed, and it becomes difficult either to imagine a life beyond capitalism or to believe in a politics that takes democracy seriously.

Religious Fundamentalism and the New Conservatism

According to Ngugi Wa Thiong'O, fundamentalisms are "at the heart of globalization" and go hand in hand with neoliberal policies as "finance capital and the elevation of the market to the status of a universal deity generate other fundamentalisms, religious and secular, either in alliance with them or in opposition."[23] The second fundamentalism now affecting the United States can be seen in the religious fervor embraced by Bush and his cohorts that substitutes blind faith and intolerance for critical reason and

social responsibility.²⁴ Under the Bush administration, the line between the state and religion is being
erased as government officials, many now proxies for
radical Christian evangelicals, embrace and impose
on American society a rigid moralism and set of values
that are largely bigoted, patriarchal, uncritical, and
insensitive to real social problems such as poverty,
racism, the crisis in health care, and the increasing
impoverishment of America's children. Instead of addressing these problems, evangelicals with enormous
political clout are waging a campaign to ban same-sex
marriages, serve up creationism instead of science,
privatize Social Security, eliminate embryonic stem
cell research, and overturn *Roe v. Wade* among other
abortion rights cases. Rampant anti-intellectualism
coupled with Taliban-like moralism boldly translate
into everyday cultural practices and state practices
as right-wing evangelicals live out their messianic
view of the world. Right-wing religious evangelicals
such as Pat Robertson, James Dobson, and Jerry
Falwell make public announcements on all manner
of public and foreign policy issues while cultivating a
close relationship with the White House. For example,
Robertson, a Bush administration favorite, has called
for the assassination of Hugo Chavez, the president
of Venezuela, and suggested that the devastating
stroke suffered by Prime Minister Ariel Sharon was
"divine punishment for pulling Israel out of Gaza last
summer."²⁵ In addition, many Christian conservatives
have played a prominent role in anointing the war
on terrorism as a "holy war" and have helped shape
the Bush administration's policies toward the Middle
East, providing further legitimation for the "war on
terrorism" and the ongoing assault on Palestinian
rights and sovereignty. The Christian Right has not
only directed its anger at Islam but has often made

public statements expressing views so extreme that they were widely reported in the Arab world, further fueling hatred of the United States and providing a recruiting tool for Islamic terrorists. Esther Kaplan provides a compilation of some of the more egregious anti-Islamic remarks. She writes:

> Franklin Graham, the son of traveling evangelist Billy Graham, whom President Bush credits with his religious awakening—the same Franklin Graham who had led Bush's inaugural prayer—denounced Islam on television as "a very evil and wicked religion." Reverend Jerry Vines, a past president of the 16–million-member Southern Baptist Convention, a religious organization with strong ties to the administration, called the Muslim prophet Muhammad a "demon-obsessed pedophile" … while Falwell's characterization of Muhammad as "a terrorist" touched off a riot in Sholapur, India, that left nine people dead and one hundred injured.[26]

These extreme views appear to be welcomed in the highest reaches of government, given the close alignment between evangelical conservatives who make up 40 percent of Bush's voting bloc and the Bible-studying neoconservative faction of the Republican Party, which includes Vice President Cheney, Defense Secretary Rumsfeld, Secretary of State Condoleezza Rice, Richard Pearle, Paul Wolfowitz, and Douglas Feith, all of whom endorse rigid moral principles and welcome the electoral support of their right-wing evangelical supporters. The new place of religious fundamentalism in American politics attempts "to collapse the spiritual into the political (making politics into a religious mission) and the spiritual into the political (making religion into a political issue)."[27] At the same time, patriotism if not political identity itself is defined as a matter of spiritual worthiness. While religious fundamentalists organize through churches and grassroots organizations, neoconservatives preserve a more secular traditionalism and organize primarily through think tanks, conservative foundations, and nongovernmental agencies. Power breeds arrogance, and the close alliance of Christian fundamentalists and neoconservative empire builders accepts as a basic truth that the United States has a duty to re-shape the world in terms of its own global interests. Moralism abroad gives rise to a "holy war" and a war for oil euphemistically served up as democracy, while Bush-style moralism at home wages a war against women's reproductive rights, undertakes to "save" Terri Schiavo, and promotes an all-out national effort to insert intelligent design in high school biology classes. For the neoconservatives, market-freedom is best secured by keeping under control people who want to hold power accountable and who oppose the revolutionary aims and ethos of the new conservatism. Neoconservatives and right-wing evangelicals occupy a world that is neatly defined into good and evil, and the rigidity that underlies such a view is supported through a notion of divine mission, a moral certainty, and a set of absolute convictions designed to view dissent and otherness as a threat to their view of economic and religious salvation. This mixing of religious and political convictions with a rigid moralism that impacts directly on those who disagree with these rigid views is evident in the fact that more and more conservative pharmacists are refusing to fill prescriptions for religious reasons. Mixing medicine, politics, and religion means that some women are being denied birth control pills or any other product designed to prevent conception. Sex education inspired by right wing evangelical institutions is promoting only abstinence, and educational information challenging these approaches is often being either disparaged or ignored. Evangelicals and neoconservative politicians across the country are passing legislation to sponsor "abstinence-only education," despite a spate of research suggesting that such programs do not work. Similarly, the Bush administration has succumbed to pressure from religious fundamentalists by eliminating information from government websites about alternative forms of birth control, citing falsified scientific information such as assertions that using the birth control pill promotes higher rates of breast cancer, and producing curricula which claim that "half of all gay male teenagers in the U.S. are HIV positive."[28]

Bush's much-exalted religious fundamentalism does more than promote a disdain for critical thought, reinforce retrograde social policies, and promote despicable forms of homophobia and patriarchy. It also undermines scientific reason, shuts down debate, and banishes criticism to the dustbin of history. On those rare occasions when the Christian Right makes an appeal to debate and dialogue, it is almost always an act of bad faith. For instance, its call to keep open the debate on global warming and intelligent design is more often than not a strategic ploy designed to evade indisputable scientific evidence that contradicts its rigid faith-based positions. Even popular culture is not immune from the Christian Right's morality squad, given that it inspires a wave of criticism and censorship against all but the most sanitized facets of the entertainment industry. What is one to make of the Christian Right's attack on children's shows that allegedly offer up homoerotic representations, such

as those attributed to the animated cartoon character SpongeBob SquarePants?[29] Prior to December 25,
2005, many Christian fundamentalists launched a
relentless attack on all the major media outlets, claiming that Christmas was under siege by all manner of
secularists and barely disguising a strong anti-Semitic
tradition that dates back to Henry Ford's infamous
1921 publication *The International Jew.* The rise and
impact of religious fundamentalism on the landscape
of American politics and culture not only represent
a "chapter of irrational hysteria in America's cultural
history" but also make visible the warm welcome that
religious extremists receive at the highest reaches of
American political power and in the dominant media,
both of which increasingly pander to alleged "people
of faith."[30] While religious extremism is an old story
in American history,[31] the current influence that
Christian fundamentalists now exercise in shaping
both domestic and foreign policy is unprecedented
and has very dangerous implications for diminishing
democracy both at home and abroad.

The Attack on Critical Thought and Dissent

The third anti-democratic dogma can be seen in the
relentless attempt on the part of the Bush administration to destroy critical education as a foundation for an
engaged citizenry and a vibrant democracy. The attack
on secular critical thought and diversity is evident in
the attempts to corporatize education, exclude poor
and minority youth, standardize curricula, privatize
public schooling, and use the language of business
as a model for governance; it is also evident in the
ongoing efforts of corporations and neoconservative
ideologues to weaken the power of university faculty,

turn full-time jobs into contractual labor, and hand over those larger educational forces in the culture to a small group of corporate interests. Higher education, too, has been attacked by right-wing ideologues such as David Horowitz and Lynne Cheney, who view it as the "weak link" in the war against terror and a potential fifth column.[32] Horowitz not only is the head of an organization that monitors left-wing professors at the national level but also acts as the figurehead for various well-funded and orchestrated conservative student groups such as the Young Americans and College Republicans, which perform the groundwork for his "Academic Bill of Rights" policy efforts that seek out juicy but rare instances of "political bias"— whatever that is or however it might be defined—in college classrooms. These efforts have resulted in considerable sums of public money being devoted to hearings in multiple state legislatures, most recently in Pennsylvania, in addition to helping impose, as the *Chronicle of Higher Education* put it, a "chilly climate" of self-policing of academic freedom and pedagogy.[33] It gets worse. At the University of California, Los Angeles (UCLA), the Bruin Alumni Association has posted on its website an article titled "The Dirty Thirty," in which it targets what it calls the university's "most radical professors."[34] "Radical," according to this group, appears to mean, among other things, holding views in opposition to the war in Iraq, supporting affirmative action, and attacking "President Bush, the Republican Party, multi-national corporations, and even our fighting men and women."[35] The group—headed by right-wing ideologue Andrew Jones, an ex-student and former chairman of UCLA's Bruin Republicans student group—has as its mission the task of exposing and combating "an exploding crisis of political radicalism on campus."[36] Jones's extremism is even too much for his old boss, Horowitz, who once fired Jones for pressuring "students to file false reports about leftists."[37] The Bruin Alumni Association does more than promote "McCarthy-like smears," intolerance, and anti-intellectualism through a vapid appeal for "balance"; it also offers $100 prizes to any students willing to provide information on their teachers' political views. Of course, this has less to do with protesting genuine demagoguery than it does with attacking any professor who might raise critical questions about the status quo or hold the narratives of power accountable.[38] Illegal and unethical spying at the national level, rather than being condemned by right-wing students such as Jones, now seems to offer yet another strategy to harass professors, insult students by treating them as if they are mindless, and provide a model for student participation in the classroom that mimics tactics similarly used by fascist and Nazi plants in the 1930s.

No longer viewed as a repository for critical thought, debate, and the shaping of an informed citizenry, higher education is increasingly being reduced to serving either the imperatives of job training or the ideological demands of patriotic conformity. But there is more at stake here than simply substituting training for education, and ideological conformity for critical learning: Higher education is also a central player in the construction of the national security state. Universities now supply resources, engage in research contracts, and accept huge amounts of defense contract money to provide the personnel, expertise, and tools necessary to expand the security imperatives of the U.S. government, and with no apologies.

If higher education is under fire, public schooling appears to have lost the war. Functioning largely as training sites for basic work skills and test preparation, public schools no longer include the discourse of equity and citizenship as central to their purpose and meaning. Either reduced in this way to training centers for middle-class kids or modeled after prisons for the urban and black poor—with an emphasis on criminalizing student behavior and prioritizing security over critical learning—schools now serve to promote a culture of conformity, character reform, consumerism, and deception, on the one hand, and to punish those deemed marginalized by virtue of class and color, on the other. No longer addressed as critical educators and responsible intellectuals, teachers are now largely reduced to deskilled technicians, depoliticized professionals, paramilitary police forces, hawkers for corporate goods, or grant writers.

Public and higher education are only two of the main sites of education under siege. Several institutions committed to public literacy such as the media and other sites that reflect the educational force of the larger culture are also under attack either for being critical or for not toeing the patriotic line. Under the sway of a market fundamentalism and government bullying, the dominant media have deteriorated into a morass of commercialism, propaganda, televangelism, and entertainment.[39] In such circumstances, the media neither operate in the interests of the public good as a fourth estate nor provide the pedagogical conditions necessary for producing critical citizens or defending a vibrant democracy. Instead, as Robert McChesney and John Nichols point out, concentrated media depoliticize the culture of politics, commercially carpet-bomb citizens, and denigrate public life.[40] Rather than performing an essential public service, they have become the primary pedagogical tool for promoting a culture of consent and conformity in which citizens are misinformed and public discourse is debased.

Engaged in a form of public pedagogy that legitimates dominant power rather than holding it accountable to the highest ethical and political standards, giant media conglomerates such as Clear Channel Communications and Rupert Murdoch's News Corporation (Fox News) have become advertising appendages for dominant political and corporate interests. Such media restrict the range of views to which people have access and thereby undermine democracy by stripping citizens of the possibility for vigorous public debate, critical exchange, and civic engagement. Even where critical thought does appear, whether in the university, the media, or other educational sites, it is often attacked and disarmed through right-wing campaigns of intimidation, appeals to fear and security in order to refuse accountability, and pernicious suggestions that such criticism is un-American or even treasonous. With such accusations, the Bush government, in its no-holds-barred war against terrorism, collapses the distinction "between enemies of the state and ordinary citizens" and, in doing so, emulates dictatorships of the latter part of the twentieth century in countries like Peru.[41] In Bush's Manichaean world of good and evil, the "appeal to absolutes blocks the road to open inquiry and genuine thinking."[42]

Along with large sections of the dominant, right wing–controlled media, the Bush-Cheney crowd repeatedly smear responsible criticisms of the war in Iraq as well as critiques of the administration's retrograde domestic polices by actually suggesting that such critics aid terrorists. The smear tactic was on display when, for instance, Paul Wolfowitz in 2004 dismissed critical reporting regarding the "raging insurgency on Iraq as 'rumors' he attributed to a Baghdad press corps too 'afraid to travel.'"[43] In an attempt to preserve its power at all costs, the Bush administration, when not denouncing critics as either irresponsible or un-American, pumps out propaganda by faking its own news, planting stories favorable to the Bush worldview at home and abroad, bribing conservative journalists like Armstrong Williams, or simply relying on Fox News to divert attention from embarrassing revelations about government incompetence, failures, misdeeds, and lies. When such efforts at manipulation and persuasion fail to work, the Bush administration gets coercive and punitive. In the event that hyperventilating appeals to fear, patriotism, and nationalism do not move the public, critics are often intimidated or punished. When the *New York Times* exposed the government use of the National Security Agency to conduct warrant-free wiretapping on American citizens, for example, Bush responded by discrediting the leak as "shameful" and called for a Justice Department investigation to locate the internal sources who exposed yet another violation of individual rights. The real crime, it seems, is the exposure of government wrongdoing, rather than the lawlessness and expression of absolute power revealed by such practices. Bush also implied that critics of his illegal wiretaps were guilty of giving aid and comfort to Al Qaeda. As an editorial in *The Nation* pointed out, if this were true "the ranks of the treasonous now include leaders of the President's own party, and the *New York Times*'s revelations of illegal wiretaps foretell an earthquake."[44] A now-infamous expression of government disdain for responsible criticism took place when the Bush administration tried to punish former ambassador Joseph Wilson (for having disclosed in a *New York Times* op-ed that a central argument of the administration's case for the Iraq War was false) by leaking the name of Wilson's wife, Valerie Plame, to conservative columnist Robert Novak, who revealed that she was a CIA operative. Right-wing ideologues and Christian evangelicals in the major broadcast media consistently label almost anyone who criticizes the war in Iraq or Bush's domestic policies either as un-American or as a traitor. In fact, such charges can be heard almost daily from religious extremists and right-wing commentators such as Pat Robertson, Bill O'Reilly, and Ann Coulter.[45] Throughout all these incidents, the Bush administration and its right-wing cheerleaders are effectively dismantling any vestige of democratic public space through which to uphold government accountability. Increasingly, the global struggle for democracy needs to recite in loud voices Hannah Arendt's eloquent warning from *Men in Dark Times:*

> If it is the function of the public realm to throw light on the affairs of men by providing a space of appearances in which they can show in deed and word, for better and worse, who they are and what they can do, then darkness has come when this light is extinguished by a "credibility gap" and "invisible government," by speech that does not disclose what is but sweeps it under the carpet, by exhortations, moral or otherwise, that, under the pretext of upholding old truths, degrade all truth to meaningless triviality.[46]

We are indeed living in dark times. As the critical power of education within various public spheres is reduced to the official discourse of compliance, conformity, and forced reverence, it becomes more difficult for the American public to engage in critical debates, link private frustrations to policy failings, and recognize the distortions and lies that underlie much of current government policies. How else to explain how Bush was reelected in 2004 in the face of flagrant lies about why the United States invaded Iraq, the passing of tax reform policies that rewarded the ultrarich at the expense of the middle and lower classes, and grandstanding over foreign policy decisions largely equated with bullying by the rest of the world? What is one to make of Bush's winning popular support for his reelection in light of his record of letting millions of young people slide into unemployment or underemployment, poverty, and hopelessness; his refusal to protect public health and the environment; his dismantling of civil liberties; and his promulgation of a culture of fear that is gutting the most cherished of American civil liberties?[47]

The Politics of Cronyism and the Return of Old-Style Racism

The attack on critical thought feeds into the reproduction of a number of anti-democratic tendencies in the United States that seem to be connected to increasingly frequent displays of unilateralism, self-interest, and outright corruption on the part of the Bush administration, which has sought to strengthen its own executive powers in addition to attacking the judiciary and undermining due process, promoting an ideology of self-reliance, and showing a blatant disregard for the international institutions and criminal courts that enforce human rights laws. Other tendencies that support the Bush administration's efforts to extend and exercise its power regardless of the consequences for democracy include the increasing reality of a one-party system that exhibits a deep disdain for pluralism and resorts to corrupt attempts at redistricting; crass manipulation of voting rules; tactics designed to intimidate oppositional voter blocs, especially minorities; and the fraudulent use of voting machines—all of which is intended to lock in a permanent Republican administration. Rampant cronyism and political corruption are exemplified in the scandal surrounding favorite-son lobbyist Jack Abramoff, the appointment of political hacks such as Michael Brown to head government agencies such as the Federal Emergency Management Agency (FEMA), the awarding of government contracts to donors who make big contributions to the Republican Party, and the placing of a number of right-wing evangelical supporters on government policymaking panels, in spite of their glaring incompetence to perform their appointed jobs. Additionally, a brutal sexism and ho-mophobia, as well as a resurgent racism, are on the rise in the United States, coupled with the language of hate and scapegoating that spews forth daily on talk radio and from infamous conservative talking heads such as Sean Hannity, Rush Limbaugh, and Michael Savage, all of whom reflect a disdain for hu-man rights and reveal something dreadful about the new narratives with which this government wants to define American culture. The war on terrorism has produced the "crudest expression of racial antipathy ... redolent of imperial and colonial domination."[48] Inside the blandest discourses of nationalism and patriotism, racist practices shape the widest dimen-sions of culture, symbolizing all "racial others" as an alleged external threat to American civilization. As I pointed out in Chapter 1, this is amply illustrated in the war against African-Americans—exemplified in the images from New Orleans after Hurricane Katrina, but perhaps even more emphatically by the fact that

70 percent of all prisoners incarcerated in the United States are people of color.

The threat to domestic order has been extended to include others from the global south who are now perceived to threaten national security. From political theorist Samuel P. Huntington, who rails against the threat of "Hispanization,"[49] to CNN television host Lou Dobbs, who believes the country is being overrun by illegal immigrants, to Pat Robertson, who publicly stated that Muslims were "worse than Nazis,"[50] there is a growing discourse of racist invective directed toward Mexican immigrants, Arabs, Muslims, and others who threaten the "civilizational" distinctiveness of American culture, take away American jobs, or allegedly support acts of terrorism directed against the United States. There is also an increase in the surveillance of citizenry, called euphemistically the "special collection program," which is being conducted outside the jurisdiction of the courts; an increase in reports of U.S. human rights abuses such as torture, kidnapping, and making people "disappear"; and the emergence of a hypernationalism fueled by racism in which immigrants are now construed as a threat to American jobs, safety, and law and order—just as the country has become more and more obsessed with national security, crime, and the increased surveillance of its citizens. Such rhetoric and practices increasingly make the United States look like the ruthless Latin American dictatorships that seized power in the 1970s, all of which appealed to fear, security, and the use of extralegal practices to defend barbaric acts of torture, abuse, and disappearance. The writer Isabel Hilton rightly invokes this repressed piece of history and what it reveals about the current Bush administration. She writes:

The delusion that office holders know better than the law is an occupational hazard of the powerful and one to which those of an imperial cast of mind are especially prone. Checks and balances—the constitutional underpinning of the democratic idea that no one individual can be trusted with unlimited power—are there to keep such delusions under control.... When disappearance became state practice across Latin America in the 70s it aroused revulsion in democratic countries where it is a fundamental tenet of legitimate government that no state actor may detain—or kill—another human being without having to answer to the law. Not only has President Bush discarded that principle, he even brags about it.[51]

The Militarization of America

Couple these particularly insidious abuses of human rights with the aforementioned anti-democratic tendencies, an expanding hypernationalism, and the emergence of fundamentalist zeal, and the elements of an ascendant authoritarianism become more visible in the United States. All of these forces gain strength through a fourth anti-democratic dogma that is shaping American life: the ongoing militarization of public life—the emergence of militarism as what David Theo Goldberg calls a "new regime of truth," a new epistemology defining what is fact and fiction, right and wrong, just and unjust. Not only are Americans obsessed with military power, but "it has become central to our national identity."[52] How else to explain the fact that the United States has "725 official military bases outside the country and 969 at home"? Or that it "spends more on 'defense' than all the rest of the world put together.... [T]his country is obsessed with war: rumors of war, images of war, 'preemptive' war, 'preventive' war, 'surgical' war, 'prophylactic' war, 'permanent' war"?[53] Bush's permanent war policy, with its unilateral legitimation of preemptive strikes against potential enemies, not only sets a dangerous precedent for ushering in authoritarianism but also encourages similarly demagogic policies among other right-wing nations. As President Bush explained at a news conference on April 13, 2004, and has repeated again and again in different public venues as 2006 has unfolded: "This country must go on the offense and stay on the offense."[54] By regarding military power as the highest expression of social truth and national greatness, the Bush administration has opened a dangerous new chapter in American military history that now gives unfettered support to what C. Wright Mills once called a "'military metaphysics'—a tendency to see international problems as military problems and to discount the likelihood of finding a solution except through military means."[55] Such aggressive militarism is fashioned out of an ideology that not only supports a foreign policy based on what Cornel West calls "the cowboy mythology of the American frontier fantasy" but also affects domestic policy as it expands "police power, augments the prison-industrial complex, and legitimizes unchecked male power (and violence) at home and in the workplace. It views crime as a monstrous enemy to be crushed (targeting poor people) rather than as an ugly behavior to change (by addressing the conditions that often encourage such behavior)."[56]

The influence of militaristic truths, values, social relations, and identities now permeates and defines American culture. Major universities, for example, aggressively court the military establishment for Defense Department research grants and in doing so become less open to academic subjects and programs that encourage rigorous debate, dialogue, and critical thinking. In fact, as higher education is pressured by both the Bush administration and its jingoistic supporters to serve the needs of the military-industrial complex, universities increasingly deepen their connections to the national security state in ways that are boldly celebrated. For instance, public institutions such as Pennsylvania State University, Carnegie-Mellon, the University of Pennsylvania, Johns Hopkins, and a host of others have shamelessly expanded the reach and influence of the national security state by entering into formal agreements with the Federal Bureau of Investigation (FBI) in order to "create a link between a leading research university and government agencies."[57] And as Graham Spanier, president of Penn State, argues in a statement pregnant with irony, the establishment of the National Security Higher Education Advisory Board, which he heads, "sends a positive message that leaders in higher education are willing to assist our nation during these challenging times."[58] Such commentary reads like a page out of George Orwell's *1984,* countering every decent and democratic value that defines higher education as a democratic public sphere. It is difficult not to view such developments cynically. Maybe Spanier can bring the power of his office and the resources of the university to solve problems associated with the FBI's enhanced program of domestic spying, provide new recruits for CIA "black sites" (torture prisons) abroad, or perhaps train technical specialists to work in the Extraordinary Rendition Program, which kidnaps alleged terrorists in foreign lands and sends them to countries less inclined to fuss over legal rights and civil liberties. Or maybe he and his fellow board members will offer the resources of the nation's great research universities to provide information on Muslim and Arab students who might pose a potential threat to the United States, not to mention those faculty and students opposed to Bush's foreign and domestic policies who allegedly pose a similar threat. On a more optimistic reading, maybe Spanier and his colleagues can provide frank critique and crucial advice to the FBI on how to handle recent revelations concerning its role in domestic spying—behavior reminiscent of its COINTELPRO days when it harassed and spied on anti-war demonstrators, civil rights activists, and other dissenters.[59]

Unfortunately, public schools fare no better in an era of permanent war. Public schools today not only have more military recruiters than before; they also have more military personnel teaching in the classrooms.[60] When the market logic of neoliberalism combines with the militaristic logic of the current administration, the purpose of schooling undergoes a fundamental shift for those populations whose labor is no longer needed. Schools now adopt the logic of "tough love" by implementing zero-tolerance policies that effectively model urban public schools after prisons, just as students' rights increasingly diminish under the onslaught of a military-style discipline.[61] Students in many schools, especially those in poor urban and rural areas, are routinely searched, frisked, subjected to involuntary drug tests, maced, and carted off to jail. The not-so-hidden curriculum here is that certain youth make a poor social investment; they can't be trusted; their actions need to be regulated preemptively; and their rights are not worth protecting. For instance, the No Child Left Behind Act requires schools to provide students' personal information to military recruiters, who then attempt to sell them on joining the armed services. Military recruiters roam the corridors of schools and are as omnipresent as guidance counselors, providing a number of school services and offering a range of gimmicks such as video-game contests and sponsored concerts in order to up their recruitment quotas. Nearly 50 percent of junior and senior high schools in the Chicago Public Schools system support Junior Reserve Officers' Training Corps (JROTC) programs, while other schools in Chicago run as military academies.[62] As a result of struggles on the recruiting front, the army went so far as to conduct a "Take It to the Streets" recruiting campaign in the spring of 2004, during which decked-out Hummers, replete with hip-hop blaring woofers and *America's Army*, a popular video game, were paraded around city centers in the hopes of persuading young African-American and Latino youth to join up. Of course, not all poor minority youth comply with such measures. For many black and brown youth and adults, incarceration has reached record levels as prison construction outstrips the construction of schools, hospitals, and other life-preserving institutions.

As Michael Hardt and Antonio Negri point out in *Multitude,* war has become the organizing principle of society and the foundation for politics and other social relations.[63] Militarism has become the most powerful form of public pedagogy, a mode of biopolitics shaping all aspects of social life, and one of its consequences is a growing authoritarianism that encourages profit-hungry monopolies, the ideology of faith-based certainty, and the undermining of any vestige of critical education, dissent, and dialogue. Education is in this case either severely narrowed and trivialized in the media or converted into training and character reform in the schools. In higher education, democracy is deemed an excess, if not a pathology, as right-wing ideologues and corporate wannabe administrators increasingly police what faculty say, teach, and do in their courses. And it is going to become worse.

Indeed, given that the Bush administration governs by "dividing the country along [the] fault lines of fear, intolerance, ignorance and religious rule,"[64] the future does not look bright for democracy, especially as it pertains to those populations now considered disposable and marginalized by virtue of class and race. Critical race theorist David Theo Goldberg correctly argues that the message of Bush's reelection boils down to this:

[D]on't get ill, lose your job, or retire; don't breathe, swim in the ocean, travel, or think critical thoughts; invest your life-savings in the stock market even though you will likely lose it all; go to community college for two years of technical training rather than to four-year universities where your mind will be turned to liberal mush; support tax cuts for the wealthy, and military service for the poor. If you step out of line, remember the Patriot Act is there to police you at home and a loaded B52 bomber hovers overhead abroad.[65]

The Struggle for an Oppositional Biopolitics

Abstracted from the ideal of public commitment, the new authoritarianism represents a political and economic practice and form of militarism that loosen the connections among substantive democracy, critical agency, and critical education. In opposition to the rising tide of authoritarianism, educators across the globe must make a case for linking learning to progressive social change while struggling to pluralize and critically engage the diverse sites where public pedagogy takes place. In part, this suggests forming alliances that can make sure every sphere of social life is recognized as an important site of the political, social, and cultural struggle that is so crucial to any attempt to forge the knowledge, identifications, affective investments, and social relations that constitute political subjects and social agents capable of energizing and spreading the basis for a substantive global democracy.

Such circumstances require that pedagogy be embraced as a moral and political practice, one that is directive and not dogmatic, an outgrowth of struggles designed to resist the increasing depoliticization of political culture that is the hallmark of the current Bush revolution. Education is the terrain where consciousness is shaped, needs are constructed, and the capacity for individual self-reflection and broad social change is nurtured and produced. Education has assumed an unparalleled significance in shaping the language, values, and ideologies that legitimatize the structures and organizations that support the imperatives of global capitalism. Efforts to reduce it to a technique or methodology notwithstanding, education remains a crucial site for the production and struggle over those pedagogical and political conditions that provide the possibilities for people to develop forms of agency that enable them individually and collectively to intervene in the processes through which the material relations of power shape the meaning and practices of their everyday lives. Within the current historical context, struggles over power take on a symbolic and discursive as well as a material and institutional form. The struggle over education is about more than the struggle over meaning and identity; it is also about *how* meaning, knowledge, and values are produced, authorized, and made operational within economic and structural relations of power. Education is not at odds with politics; it is a crucial element in any definition of the political, offering not only the theoretical tools for a systematic critique of authoritarianism but also a language of possibility for creating actual movements for democratic social change and a new oppositional biopolitics that affirms life rather than death, shared responsibility rather than shared fears, and engaged citizenship rather than the stripped-down values of consumerism. At stake here is combining symbolic forms and processes conducive to democratization with broader social contexts and the institutional formations of power itself. The key objective is to understand and engage educational and pedagogical practices from the point of view of how they are bound up with larger relations of power. Educators, students, and parents need to be clearer about how power works through and in texts, representations, and discourses, while at the same time recognizing that power cannot be limited to the study of representations and discourses, even at the level of public policy. Changing consciousness is not the same as altering the institutional basis of oppression; at the same time, institutional reform cannot take place without a change in consciousness capable of recognizing not only injustice but also the very possibility for reform—and of reinventing the conditions and practices that make a more just future possible. In addition, it is crucial to raise questions about the relationship between pedagogy and civic culture, on the one hand, and what it takes for individuals and social groups to believe that they have any responsibility whatsoever to even address the realities of class, race, gender, and other specific forms of domination, on the other hand. For too long, progressives have ignored the fact that the strategic dimension of politics is inextricably connected to questions of critical education and pedagogy, to what it means to acknowledge that education is always tangled up with power, ideologies, values, and the acquisition of particular forms of agency as well as specific visions of the future. The primacy of critical pedagogy to politics, social change, and the radical imagination in such dark times is dramatically captured by the internationally renowned sociologist Zygmunt Bauman. He writes:

> Adverse odds may be overwhelming, and yet a democratic (or, as Cornelius Castoriadis would say, an autonomous) society knows of no substitute for education and self-education as a means to influence the turn of events that can be squared with its own nature, while that nature cannot be preserved for long without "critical pedagogy"—an education sharpening its critical edge, "making society feel guilty" and "stirring things up" through stirring human consciences. The fates of freedom, of democracy that makes it possible while being made possible by it, and of education that breeds dissatisfaction with the level of both freedom and democracy achieved thus far, are inextricably connected and not to be detached from one another. One may view that intimate connection as another specimen of a vicious circle—but it is within that circle that human hopes and the chances of humanity are inscribed, and can be nowhere else.[66]

Fortunately, power is never completely on the side of domination, religious fanaticism, or political corruption. Neither is it entirely in the hands of those who view democracy as an excess or burden. Educators need to develop a new discourse and a revitalized positive notion of an oppositional global biopolitics whose aim is to foster a democratic pedagogy and political culture that embody the legacy and principles of social justice, equality, freedom, and rights associated with democratic notions of time, space, pluralism, power, discourse, identities, morality, and the future. But such a politics cannot be simply nation-based. If it is to be effective, it has to find ways to globalize both justice and resistance, use the new media as critical pedagogical tools, and form new alliances among various oppositional movements, taking seriously pedagogy as a political practice that crosses borders, affirms difference, and generates new international alliances in the struggle for new public spaces. Arif Dirlik argues that any viable notion of oppositional biopolitics has to address the very real problems of global modernity and its legacies of class and inequality.[67] Dirlik's brilliant work on the importance of place, space, and colonialism, on the one hand, and the need for forging new struggles on a transnational level, on the other, raises important questions about the meaning of oppositional biopolitics not merely as an ontological matter but as a concrete issue of history, power, and struggle. In light of such a challenge, more and more individuals and movements at home and around the globe—including students, workers, feminists, educators, writers, environmentalists, senior citizens, artists, and a host of others—are organizing to challenge the dangerous slide on the part of the United States into the dark abyss of an authoritarianism that threatens not just the *promise* but the very *idea* of global democracy in the twenty-first century.

The aftermath of Hurricane Katrina provided a glimpse of the dire consequences that can befall a society when it succumbs to the notions that neoliberal capitalism and democracy are synonymous, that the highest values in society can be measured only in economic terms, and that some groups in society are disposable because they are not productive consumers. The ideas of justice and democracy are under siege, just as democratic politics and values appear to be relegated to the back burner of individual and social agency. But justice and a substantive democracy are far too important to disappear under the force of the new religious, militaristic, and economic fundamentalisms that govern America. We may live in dark times, as Hannah Arendt reminds us, but history is open and the space of the possible is larger than the one on display. The tragedy of Katrina demands a new politics, language, and sense of civic courage. Jacques Derrida touched on the political task ahead when he stated, "We must do the impossible, we must do and think the impossible. If only the possible happened, nothing more would happen. If I only did what I can do, I wouldn't do anything."[68] Clearly, it is time for those who care about an inclusive democracy to get beyond moral outrage, critique, and compassion—it is time to act, organize collectively, intervene, and reclaim the promise of a world that obliterates those political, economic, and social conditions that produced the human suffering on display not only in New Orleans but in many parts of the world.

◊

Notes

Notes to Chapter 1

1. Shaila Dewan, "How Photos Became an Icon of the Civil Rights Movement," *New York Times* (August 28, 2005). Available online at http://www.wehaitians.com/how%20photos%20became%20icon%20of%20civil%20rights%20movement.html.

2. Douglas Kellner, *The Persian Gulf TV War* (Boulder: Westview, 1992).

3. This practice was later changed. See Editorial, "Return of the Fallen," *National Security Archive* (April 28, 2005). Available online at www.gwu.edu/~nsarchiv/NSAEBB/NSAEBB152/.

4. The relationship here to a fascist aesthetics is obvious, and I have taken up the relationship between such an aesthetics and the Bush administration in Henry Giroux, *Beyond the Spectacle of Terrorism* (Boulder: Paradigm Publishers, 2006). On the relationship between the spectacle and the first Gulf War, see Douglas Kellner, *Persian Gulf TV War* and *Media Spectacle and the Crisis of Democracy* (Boulder: Paradigm Publishers, 2004).

5. Bill Moyers, "The Media, Politics, and Censorship," *Common Dreams News Center* (May 10, 2004). Available online at http://www.commondreams.org/views04/0510–10.htm.

6. Cited in Frank Rich, "The War's Lost Weekend," *New York Times* (May 29, 2004), pp. AR1, 8.

7. Cited in Eric Alterman, "Is Koppel a Commie?" *The Nation* (May 24, 2004), p. 10.

8. Seymour M. Hersh, *Chain of Command: The Road from 9/11 to Abu Ghraib* (New York: Harper Perennial, 2005).

9. David Simpson, "The Mourning Paper," *London Review of Books* 26:10 (May 20, 2004). Available online at www.lrb.co.uk/v26/n10/print/simp01_.html.

10. An interesting set of essays on the Rodney King affair can be found in Robert Gooding-Williams, ed., *Reading Rodney King/Reading Urban Uprisings* (New York: Routledge, 1993).

11. Simpson, "The Mourning Paper."

12. It is worth noting how the media coverage of the war in Iraq and of Hurricane Katrina differs when viewed from the contrasting perspectives of a "natural catastrophe" and the ensuing man-made "social debacle." Labeled as a natural disaster, Katrina seemed removed from the political realm and social criticism until it became clear, in the aftermath of the tragedy, that matters of race and class had to be addressed. The "natural" aspect of the disaster opened the door for media coverage of a domestic tragedy that could articulate dissent in a way that the state-manufactured war coverage could not. In other words, natural catastrophes are not supposed to be politicized in themselves; it was only in the aftermath that the emergence of racial and class politics enabled the media and the public to criticize the negligence and incompetence of the government; and because the event occurred on domestic soil, the government had less control over the way the media constructed the event, particularly in invoking issues related to poverty, race, and inequality. I want to thank Grace Pollock for this insight.

13. Dan Frosch, "Back from the Dead," *ALTWeeklies. com* (September 28, 2005), pp. 1–3. Available online at http://www.altweeklies.com/gyrobase/AltWeeklies/Story?oid=oid%3A151104.

14. Dan Barry, "Macabre Reminder: The Corpse on Union Street," *New York Times* (September 8, 2005), pp. 1–3. Available online at http://query.nytimes.com/gst/fullpage.html?res=9C02EEDD1331F93AA3575AC0A9639C8B63.

15. Ibid.

16. Cited in Derrick Z. Jackson, "Healthcare Swept Away," *Boston Globe* (September 21, 2005). Available online at http://www.boston.com.

17. Rosa Brooks, "Our Homegrown Third World," *Los Angeles Times* (September 7, 2005), pp. 1–2. Available online at http://www.commondreams.org/cgi-bin/print.cgi?file=/views05/0907–24.htm.

18. Cited in Terry M. Neal, "Hiding Bodies Won't Hide the Truth," *Washington Post* (September 8, 2005). Available online at http://www.washingtonpost.com.

19. For a brilliant analysis of the racial state, see David Theo Goldberg, *The Racial State* (Malden: Blackwell Publishing, 2001).

20. Eric Foner, "Bread, Roses, and the Flood," *The Nation* (October 3, 2005), p. 8.

21. For the most important theoretical work on the politics of disposability, see Zygmunt Bauman, *Wasted Lives* (London: Polity Press, 2004). On matters of class and disposability in America, see Louis Vehitelle, *The Disposable American* (New York: Knopf, 2006). See also Mike Davis, *Planet of Slums* (London: Verso, 2006).

22. Janet Pelz, "The Poor Shamed Us into Seeing Them," *Seattle Post-Intelligencer* (September 19, 2005), pp. 1–2. Available online at http://www.commondreams.org/cgi-bin/print.cgi?file=/views05/0919–26.htm.

23. Ruth Conniff, "Drowning the Beast," *The Progressive* (September 7, 2005). Available online at http://www.commondreams.org/views05/0907–30.htm.

24. See Michel Foucault, *The History of Sexuality: An Introduction* (New York: Vintage Books, 1990); Michel Foucault, *Society Must Be Defended: Lectures at the College*

de France 1975–1976 (New York: Picador, 1997); Giorgio Agamben, *Homo Sacer: Sovereign Power and Bare Life,* trans. Daniel Heller-Roazen (Stanford: Stanford University Press, 1998); Giorgio Agamben, *Remnants of Auschwitz: The Witness and the Archive,* trans. Daniel Heller-Roazen (Cambridge: Zone Books, 2002); Giorgio Agamben, *State of Exception,* trans. Kevin Attell (Chicago: University of Chicago, 2003); Michael Hardt and Antonio Negri, *Empire* (Cambridge: Harvard University Press, 2000); Michael Hardt and Antonio Negri, *Multitude: War and Democracy in the Age of Empire* (New York: Penguin, 2004).

25. Mitchell Dean, "Four Theses on the Powers of Life and Death," *Contretemps* 5 (December 2004), p. 17.

26. Foucault, *Society Must Be Defended,* p. 249.

27. Ibid., p. 247.

28. Mika Ojakangas, "Impossible Dialogue on Bio-Power: Agamben and Foucault," *Foucault Studies* 2 (May 2005), p. 6.

29. Foucault, *History of Sexuality,* p. 136.

30. Foucault, *Society Must Be Defended,* p. 255.

31. Ibid., p. 258.

32. Hardt and Negri, *Multitude,* p. 146.

33. Ibid., pp. xiv–xv.

34. Ibid., p. 334.

35. Paul Rabinow and Nikolas Rose, "Thoughts on the Concept of Biopower Today," paper presented at a conference on "Vital Politics: Health, Medicine and Bioeconomics of the Twenty-First Century" at the London School of Economics (September 2003), pp. 1–25. Available online at http://www.molsci.org/files/Rose_Rabinow_Biopower_Today.pdf.

36. Ibid.

37. Dean, "Four Theses," p. 17.

38. Ojakangas, "Impossible Dialogue," p. 5.

39. Hardt and Negri, *Empire,* p. 23.

40. Hardt and Negri, *Multitude,* p. 67.

41. See Agamben, *Homo Sacer, Remnants of Auschwitz,* and *State of Exception.*

42. See, especially, Agamben, *Homo Sacer,* p. 8.

43. Zygmunt Bauman, *Liquid Love* (London: Polity Press, 2003), p. 133.

44. Malcolm Bull, "States Don't Really Mind Their Citizens Dying (Provided They Don't All Do It at Once): They Just Don't Like Anyone Else to Kill Them," *London Review of Books* (December 16, 2004), p. 3.

45. Rabinow and Rose, "Thoughts on the Concept of Biopower."

46. Catherine Mills, "Agamben's Messianic Biopolitics: Biopolitics, Abandonment and Happy Life," *Contretemps* 5 (December 2004), p. 47.

47. Nicholas Mirzoeff, *Watching Babylon: The War in Iraq and Global Visual Culture* (New York: Routledge, 2005), p. 145.

48. Bauman, *Liquid Love,* p. 136.

49. Rosa Linda Fregoso, "'We Want Them Alive!': The Politics and Culture of Human Rights," *Social Identities* 12:2 (March 2006), p. 109.

50. See, for instance, Henry A. Giroux, *Against the New Authoritarianism* (Winnipeg: Arbeiter Ring Publishing, 2005).

51. Achille Mbembe, "Necropolitics," trans. Libby Meintjes, *Public Culture* 15:1 (2003), p. 16.

52. Rabinow and Rose, "Thoughts on the Concept of Biopower."

53. Foucault, *Society Must Be Defended,* p. 258.

54. There are a number of important works on the politics of neoliberalism. I have found the following particularly useful: Anatole Anton, Milton Fisk, and Nancy Holmstrom, eds., *Not for Sale: In Defense of Public Goods* (Boulder: Westview Press, 2000); Zygmunt Bauman, *Work, Consumerism and the New Poor* (London: Polity, 1998); Ulrich Beck, *Individualization* (London: Sage, 2002); Pierre Bourdieu,

Acts of Resistance: Against the Tyranny of the Market (New York: The New Press, 1998); Pierre Bourdieu, "The Essence of Neoliberalism," *Le Monde Diplomatique* (December 1998), available online at http://www.en.monde-diplomatique.fr/1998/12/08bourdieu; Pierre Bourdieu, *Firing Back: Against the Tyranny of the Market 2*, trans. Loic Wacquant (New York: The New Press, 2003); Noam Chomsky, *Profit Over People: Neoliberalism and the Global Order* (New York: Seven Stories Press, 1999); Jean Comaroff and John L. Comaroff, *Millennial Capitalism and the Culture of Neoliberalism* (Durham: Duke University Press, 2000); Lisa Duggan, *The Twilight of Equality: Neoliberalism, Cultural Politics, and the Attack on Democracy* (Boston: Beacon Press, 2003); Henry A. Giroux, *The Terror of Neoliberalism* (Boulder: Paradigm Publishers, 2004); David Harvey, *The New Imperialism* (Oxford: Oxford University Press, 2003); David Harvey, *A Brief History of Neoliberalism* (Oxford: Oxford University Press, 2005); Doug Henwood, *After the New Economy* (New York: The New Press, 2003); Colin Leys, *Market-Driven Politics* (London: Verso, 2001); Randy Martin, *Financialization of Daily Life* (Philadelphia: Temple University Press, 2002); Neil Smith, *The Endgame of Globalization* (New York: Routledge, 2005); Alain Touraine, *Beyond Neoliberalism* (London: Polity Press, 2001).

55. William DiFazio, "Katrina and President George W. Bush Forever," *Situations* 1:2 (2006), p. 87.

56. Mbembe, "Necropolitics," p. 40.

57. Zygmunt Bauman, *Wasted Lives* (London: Polity Press, 2004), p. 13.

58. For a different view of the larger politics behind Katrina, though one that I think is far too narrow, see Iris Young, "Katrina: Too Much Blame, Not Enough Responsibility," *Dissent* (Winter 2006), pp. 41–46.

59. Zygmunt Bauman, "The Horror of the Unmanageable," unpublished paper, February 2006, 25 pp.

60. Zygmunt Bauman has brilliantly developed this in-

sightful position in a number of books. See, especially, *Wasted Lives: Globalization: The Human Consequences* (New York: Columbia University Press, 2000); *Liquid Modernity* (London: Polity Press, 2000); and *Liquid Life* (London: Polity, 2005).

61. Paul Krugman, "Tragedy in Black and White," *New York Times* (September 19, 2005), p. A27.

62. Pelz, "The Poor."

63. Andrew J. Bacevich, *The New American Militarism* (New York: Oxford University Press, 2005); Kevin Baker, "We're in the Army Now: The G.O.P.'s Plan to Militarize Our Culture," *Harper's Magazine* (October 2003), p. 40.

64. See, for example, David A. Gabbard and Kenneth Saltman, eds., *Education as Enforcement* (New York: Routledge, 2003); and Randall R. Beger, "Expansion of Police Power in Public Schools and the Vanishing Rights of Students," *Social Justice* 29:1–2 (2002), pp. 119–130.

65. Tony Judt, "The New World Order," *New York Review of Books* 11:12 (July 14, 2005), p. 16.

66. Richard H. Kohn, "Using the Military at Home: Yesterday, Today, and Tomorrow," *Chicago Journal of International Law* 94:1 (Spring 2003), pp. 165–192; Catherine Lutz, "Making War at Home in the United States: Militarization and the Current Crisis," *American Anthropologist* 104:3 (2002), pp. 723–735.

67. Nicholas Mirzoeff, *Watching Babylon*, p. 16.

68. Ibid., p. 17.

69. Mbembe, "Necropolitics," pp. 11–12.

70. Bauman, *Wasted Lives; Liquid Lives;* and *Liquid Modernity.*

71. William Greider, "The Right's Grand Ambition: Rolling Back the 20th Century," *The Nation* (May 12, 2003), p. 17. As Greider puts it, "'Leave me alone' is an appealing slogan, but the Right regularly violates its own guiding principle. The antiabortion folks intend to use government power to force their own moral values on the private lives of others. Free-market right-wingers fall silent when Bush and Congress intrude to

bail out airlines, insurance companies, banks—whatever sector finds itself in desperate need. The hard-right conservatives are downright enthusiastic when the Supreme Court and Bush's Justice Department hack away at our civil liberties. The 'school choice' movement seeks not smaller government but a vast expansion of taxpayer obligations."

72. Bauman, *Wasted Lives*, p. 27.

73. Zygmunt Bauman cited in Nicholas Fearn, "NSProfile: Zygmunt Bauman," *New Statesman* (January 16, 2006), p. 30.

74. Zygmunt Bauman, *In Search of Politics* (Stanford: Stanford University Press, 1999), pp. 68–69.

75. Ibid., p. 6.

76. Ibid., pp. 12, 40.

77. Mirzoeff, *Watching Babylon*, p. 121.

78. Bauman, *Wasted Lives*, pp. 58–59.

79. Jean Comaroff and John L. Comaroff, "Millennial Capitalism: First Thoughts on a Second Coming," *Public Culture* 12:2 (2000), pp. 299, 305.

80. Cited in Thom Hartmann, "You Can't Govern If You Don't Believe in Government," *Common Dreams News Center* (September 6, 2005). Available online at http://www.commondreams.org/views05/0906–21.htm.

81. Cited in Erica Lasdon and Kyle Mantyla, *Upper Brackets: The Right's Tax Cut Boosters* (Washington, D.C.: People for the American Way Foundation, 2004). Available online at http://www.pfaw.org/pfaw/dfiles/file_281.pdf.

82. Ruth Conniff, "Drowning the Beast," *The Progressive* (September 7, 2005), p. 1.

83. Cited in Paul Krugman "Hey Lucky Duckies," *New York Times* (December 3, 2002), p. 31.

84. Robert Scheer, "The Real Costs of a Culture of Greed," *AlterNet* (September 6, 2005), p. 2. Available online at http://www.alternet.org/module/printversion/25095.

85. Judd Legum, Faiz Shakir, Nico Pitney, Amanda Terkel, Payson Schwin, and Christy Harvey, "Budget: After

Katrina, More of the Same," *Think Progress.Org* (October 21, 2005). Available online at http://www.americanprogressaction.org/site/apps/nl/content2.asp?c=klLWJcP7H&b=914257&ct=1520271.

86. Jonathan Weisman, "Budget Plan Assumes Too Much, Demands Too Little," *Washington Post* (February 7, 2007), p. A10.

87. Nicholas D. Kristof, "The Larger Shame," *New York Times* (September 6, 2005), p. 1.

88. Robert Scheer, "Does Bush Finally See Poor People?" *Common Dreams News Center* (September 20, 2005). Available online at http://www.commondreams.org/views05/0920–28.htm.

89. Judd Legum, Faiz Shakir, Nico Pitney, Amanda Terkel, Payson Schwin, and Christy Harvey, "Poverty: A Close Look at 'The Other America,'" *Think Progress.Org* (September 19, 2005). Available online at http://www.americanprogressaction.org/site/apps/nl/content2.asp?c=klLWJcP7H&b=914257&ct=1428461.

90. Robert Scheer, "Rotten Fruit of the 'Reagan Revolution,'" *Robert Scheer.com* (September 6, 2005). Available online at http://www.commondreams.org/views05/0906–23.htm.

91. Peter Dreier, "Katrina in Perspective: The Disaster Raises Key Questions About the Role of Government in American Society," *Dissent Magazine* (Summer 2005). Available online at www.dissentmagazine.org/menutest/articles/su05/dreier.htm.

92. Lewis Lapham, "The Simple Life," *Harper's Magazine* (December, 2005), p. 11.

93. William Greider, "Defining a New 'New Deal,'" *The Nation* (September 21, 2005). Available online at http://www.alternet.org/module/printversion/25745.

94. David Theo Goldberg, "(W)hacked to pieces: Devastating America," *OpenDemocracy* (September 8, 2005). Available online at http://www.opendemocracy.net/home/index.jsp.

95. Cited in Paul Krugman, "A Can't-Do Government," *New York Times* (September 2, 2005). Available online at http://www.commondreams.org/views05/0902–22.htm.

96. David Sirota, "Welcome to New Orleans," *In These Times* (October 24, 2005), p. 18.

97. Ibid., pp. 20–21.

98. Ibid., p. 21.

99. Frank Rich notes the revealing similarity between George W. Bush's "I don't think anyone anticipated the breach of levees" and Condoleezza Rice's post-9/11 claim "I don't think anybody could have predicted that these people could take an airplane and slam it into the World Trade Center." See Frank Rich, "Fallujah Floods the Superdome," *New York Times* (September 4, 2005), p. 10.

100. Spenser S. Husu and Linton Weeks, "Video Shows Bush Being Warned on Katrina," *Washington Post* (March 2, 2006), p. A01.

101. Mike Allen, "President Bush: Living Too Much in the Bubble?" *Time Magazine* (September 1, 2005). Available online at http://www.dscc.org/news/latest/20050911_bushinbubble/.

102. This is not an argument being made only by critics on the Left. Francis Fukuyama, one of the stars of the neoconservative movement, has recently jumped ship and argued in the *New York Times* that neoconservatism increasingly resembles Leninism and that "as both a political symbol and a body of thought, it has evolved into something he can no longer support." See Fukuyama, "After Neoconservatism," *New York Times Sunday Magazine* (February 19, 2006). Available online at http://www.nytimes.com/2006/02/19/magazine/neo.html?_r=1&oref=slogin.

103. Michael Eric Dyson, *Come Hell or High Water: Hurricane Katrina and the Color of Disaster* (New York: Basic, 2006), p. 25.

104. Michael Ignatieff, "The Broken Contract," *New York Times Magazine* (September 25, 2005), p. 15.

105. Bob Herbert, "A Failure of Leadership," *New York Times* (September 6, 2005). Available online at http://www.truthout.org/docs_2005/090505X.shtml.

106. James Carroll, "Katrina's Truths," *Boston Globe* (September 5, 2005). Available online at http://www.boston.com/news/globe/editorial_opinion/oped/articles/2005/09/05/katrinas_truths/.

107. Terry Lynn Karl, "Bush's Second Gulf Disaster," *OpenDemocracy* (September 7, 2005). Available online at www.opendemocracy.net/xml/xhtml/articles/2808.html.

108. Shaila Dewan, "Hotel Aid Ends, Sending Evacuees in Search of Shelter," *New York Times* (February 14, 2006). Available online at www.nytimes.com/2006/02/14/national/nationalspecial/14hotels.html.

109. Associated Press, "Audits Show Millions in Katrina Aid Wasted," *New York Times* (February 13, 2006). Available online at www.nytimes.com/aponline/national/AP-Katrina-Fraud.html.

110. Shaila Dewan, "For Want of Money, Remains of Some Hurricane Victims Not Collected," *New York Times* (February 14, 2006). Available online at www.nytimes.com/2006/02/17/national/nationalspecial/17bodies.html.

111. Cited in Spencer S. Hsu, "Katrina Report Spreads Blame," *Washington Post* (February 12, 2006), p. A01. The full White House report on Katrina, *The Federal Response to Hurricane Katrina: Lessons Learned,* is available online at http://www.whitehouse.gov/reports/katrina-lessons-learned/index.html.

112. Godfrey Hodgson, "After Katrina, a Government Adrift," *OpenDemocracy* (September 6, 2005), p. 2.

113. Margaret Thatcher delivered these words while talking to *Women's Own* magazine on October 31, 1987. The transcript is online at http://briandeer.com/social/thatcher-society.htm.

114. Bourdieu, *Firing Back.*

115. For an analysis of how the political state has been

transformed into the corporate state, see Noreena Hertz, *The Silent Takeover: Global Capitalism and the Death of Democracy* (New York: The Free Press, 2001).

116. Cited in Sean D. Hamill, "Santorum Retreats on Evacuation Penalty Remarks," *Pittsburgh Post-Gazette* (September 7, 2005). Available online at http://www.post-gazette.com/pg/05250/566844.stm.

117. Cited in Editorial, "Barbara Bush Calls Evacuees Better Off," *New York Times* (September 7, 2005). Available online at http://www.nytimes.com/2005/09/07/national/nationalspecial/07barbara.html?ex=1140498000&en=61560581b40ea782&ei=5070.

118. John Nichols, "Barbara Bush: It's Good Enough for the Poor," *The Nation* (September 7, 2005). Available online at http://www.thenation.com/blogs/thebeat?bid=1&pid=20080.

119. Cited in Bob Norman, "Savage Station," *Miami New Times* (September 22, 2005). Available online at www.miaminewtimes.com/Issues/2005–09–022/news/metro4.html.

120. Cited in ibid.

121. The audio clip of Fox News host Bill O'Reilly's comments broadcast September 13, 2005, on *The Radio Factor* can be found at *Media Matters for America*. Available online at http://mediamatters.org/items/200509150001.

122. Bob Faw, "Katrina Exposes New Orleans' Deep Poverty: Media Images of Looters Shed Light on City's Issues Regarding Race, Class," *MSNBC.com* (September 1, 2005). Available online at http://msnbc.com/id/9163091.

123. See Susan J. Douglas, "The Margins Go Mainstream," *In These Times* (October 24, 2005), p. 15.

124. Michelle Malkin, "Katrina: Hell Breaking Loose," *Michelle Malkin Blog* (August 30, 2005). Available online at http://michellemalkin.com/archives/003438.htm.

125. Peggy Noonan, "After the Storm—Hurricane Katrina: The Good, the Bad, and the Let's-Shoot-Them-Now," *Wall Street Journal* (September 1, 2005). Available online

at http://www.opinionjournal.com/columnists/pnoonan/ ?id=110007187.

126. Matt Welch, "The Deadly Bigotry of Low Expectations? Did the Rumor Mill Help Kill Katrina Victims?" *ReasonOnline* (September 6, 2005). Available online at www. reason.com/links090605.shtml.

127. Cited in ibid.

128. See Office of the Secretary of Homeland Security, "Press Conference with Officials from the Department of Homeland Security, Justice Department, Defense Department, the National Guard Bureau, U.S. Coast Guard and FEMA" (September 1, 2005). Available online at http:// www.dhs.gov/dhspublic/display?content=4779.

129. Tim Wise, "Framing the Poor: Katrina, Conservative Myth-Making and the Media," *CounterPunch* (October 27, 2005). Available online at http://www.counterpunch. org/wise10292005.html.

130. Mike Davis and Anthony Fontenot, "Hurricane Gumbo," *The Nation* (November 7, 2005), p. 15.

131. Slavoj Zizek, "The Subject Supposed to Loot and Rape: Reality and Fantasy in New Orleans," *In These Times* (October 20, 2005). Available online at www.inthesetimes. com/site/main/article/2361/.

132. Ibid.

133. Jordan Flaherty and Tamika Middleton, "Imprisoned in New Orleans," *ColorLines* (Spring 2006), p. 20.

134. Eric Klinenberg points out that "[b]eginning with the Crime Bill in 1994, all levels of government have delegated traditional social service responsibilities to paramilitary or military organizations—responsibilities that in many cases they are poorly suited to handle.... [Moreover,] they are often designed to operate behind closed doors, and much of the work they do is classified and not subject to public scrutiny." See Jeff Bleifuss's interview with Eric Klinenberg in "Disasters: Natural and Social," *In These Times* (October 24, 2005), p. 22.

135. Jean and John Comaroff, "Criminal Obsessions, After Foucault: Postcoloniality, Policing, and the Metaphysics of Disorder," *Critical Inquiry* 30 (Summer 2004), pp. 808, 804.

136. James Petras, "Mass Media and New Orleans: From Victims to Vandals," *CounterPunch* (September 17–18, 2005). Available online at http://www.counterpunch.org/petras09172005.html.

137. Brian Williams for MSNBC (September 18, 2005). Available online at http://www.msnbc.msn.com/id/934188/#050916.

138. Jeremy Scahill, "Blackwater Down," *The Nation* (October 10, 2005). Available online at http://www.thenation.com/doc/20051010/scahill.

139. Cited in ibid.

140. Cited in Amanda Marcotte, "The Shame of Blaming the Victims," *AlterNet* (September 16, 2005). Available online at http://www.alternet.org/story/25549/.

141. Cited in Jeremy Scahill, "The Militarization of New Orleans: Jeremy Scahill Reports from Louisiana," *DemocracyNow* (September 16, 2005). Available online at http://www.democracynow.org/article.pl?sid=05/09/16/1222257.

142. Mike Davis, "Who Is Killing New Orleans?" *The Nation* (April 10, 2006), p. 12.

143. Jesse Jackson, "Hurricane Looting Not Over Yet," *Chicago Sun-Times* (September 13, 2005). Available online at www.commondreams.org/cgi-bin/print.cgi?file=/views05/0913–32htm.

144. Office of the Press Secretary, "President Discusses Hurricane Katrina Relief in Address to Nation," The White House (September 15, 2005). Available online at http://www.whitehouse.gov/news/releases/2005/09/20050915–8.html.

145. Ralph Nader, "Bush's Crony Capitalism: Unaccountable, Inaudible & Out of Control," *Common Dreams News Center* (October 8, 2005). Available online at http://www.commondreams.org/views05/1008–28.htm.

146. The 2007 federal budget plan contains $39 billion in direct cuts, including $16 billion in student loans, $4.9 billion from Medicare and the State Children's Health Insurance program; housing for low-income elderly will be cut by 26 percent below the 2006 level; aid for low-income people with disabilities will face a 50 percent cut; and Child Care and Development Block Grants face $1 billion in cuts over five years. The budget also includes a cut of $17 million from child support enforcement. See Linda Feldmann, "Who Will Feel Budget's Impact?" *Christian Science Monitor* (February 8, 2006). Available online at www.csmonitor.com/2006/0208/p01s03–usec.html.

147. Scahill, "The Militarization of New Orleans."

148. James Dao, "In New Orleans, Smaller May Mean Whiter," *New York Times* (January 22, 2006), p. A19.

149. Dorothy Stukes, "Rebuilding New Orleans," *New York Times* (January 21, 2006), p. A22.

150. Cited in Petula Dvorak, "Hurricane Victims Demand More Help," *Washington Post* (February 9, 2006), p. A12.

151. On the future of the lower Ninth Ward, see Daisy Hernandez, "The Future of the Ninth Ward," *ColorLines* (Spring 2006), pp. 29–30.

152. Goldberg, "(W)hacked to Pieces."

153. For an incisive commentary on the rebuilding efforts in New Orleans, see Mike Davis, "Who Is Killing New Orleans?" *The Nation* (April 10, 2006), pp. 11–20.

154. This issue is explored in great detail in Hardt and Negri, *Multitude.*

155. Jorge Mariscal, "Lethal and Compassionate: The Militarization of U.S. Culture," *CounterPunch* (May 30, 2003). Available online at www.counterpunch.org/mariscal105052003.html.

156. Bauman, *Liquid Modernity.*

157. Cited in Hannah Arendt, "Introduction: Walter Benjamin, 1892–1940," in Walter Benjamin, *Illuminations,* trans. Harry Zohn (New York: Shocken, 1968), p. 19.

158. Mr. Arar was tortured by Syrian officials, "kept caged for a year like a nocturnal animal in an unlit, underground rat-infested cell. Then he was let go. No connection between Mr. Arar and terrorism has ever been made." See Bob Herbert, "The Destroyers," *New York Times* (February 13, 2005), p. A23.

159. Horowitz cited in Olivia Ward, "Still the Enemy," *Toronto Star* (February 19, 2006), p. D1. See also David Horowitz, *The Art of Political War and Other Radical Pursuits* (Dallas: Spence Publishing, 2000).

160. Robert L. Ivie, "Evil Enemy Versus Agonistic Other: Rhetorical Constructions of Terrorism," *The Review of Education, Pedagogy, and Cultural Studies* 25:3 (July-September 2003), p. 183.

161. Stanley Aronowitz, "Is It Time for a New Radical Party?" *Situations* 1:2 (2006), pp. 157–158.

162. Theodor Adorno, *Critical Models: Interventions and Catchwords,* trans. Henry W. Pickford (New York: Columbia University Press, 1998), pp. 292–293.

163. Edward Said, *Humanism and Democratic Criticism* (New York: Columbia University Press, 2004), p. 22.

164. See, for instance, this important work: Lewis Gordon and Jane Gordon, eds., *Not Only the Master's Tools: African-American Studies in Theory and Practice* (Boulder: Paradigm Publishers, 2006).

165. Paul Gilroy, *Postcolonial Melancholia* (New York: Columbia University Press, 2005), pp. 146–147.

166. Bauman, *Liquid Love,* p. 14.

167. Hannah Arendt, *Men in Dark Times* (New York: Harcourt, Brace & World, 1955), p. 4.

168. Bauman, *Liquid Love,* p. 125.

169. Mark Poster, *What's the Matter with the Internet?* (Minneapolis: University of Minnesota Press, 2001).

170. Hannah Arendt, *Totalitarianism: Part Three of the Origins of Totalitarianism* (New York: Harcourt, 1976), p. 162.

171. See, especially, Cornelius Castoriadis, "The Greek Polis and the Creation of Democracy," *Philosophy, Politics, Autonomy: Essays in Political Philosophy* (New York: Oxford University Press, 1991), pp. 81–123.

172. Richard J. Bernstein, *The Abuse of Evil* (London: Polity Press, 2005), p. 5.

Notes to Chapter 2

1. Sidney Blumenthal, "Bush's War on Professionals," *Salon.com* (January 5, 2006). Available online at http://www.salon.com/opinion/blumenthal/2006/01/05/spying/index.html?x.

2. Frank Rich, "I Saw Jackie Mason Kissing Santa Claus," *New York Times* (December 25, 2005), Late Edition, p. 8.

3. Paul Gilroy, *Against Race: Imagining Political Culture Beyond the Color Line* (Cambridge, Mass.: Harvard University Press, 2000), p. 148.

4. Michael Hardt and Antonio Negri, *Multitude: War and Democracy in the Age of Empire* (New York: The Penguin Press, 2004), p. 13.

5. Giorgio Agamben, "On Security and Terror," trans. Soenke Zehle, *Frankfurter Allgemeine Zeitung* (September 20, 2001). Available online at http://www.egs.edu/faculty/agamben/agamben-on-security-and-terror.html.

6. Ibid., p. 193.

7. David Harvey, *A Brief History of Neoliberalism* (New York: Oxford University Press, 2005), pp. 160–164.

8. See ibid., pp. 184–185. On disposable populations, see Zygmunt Bauman, *Wasted Lives* (London: Polity, 2004).

9. Of course, the relationship between sovereignty and death is further extended in the work of Giorgio Agamben. See, especially, his *Homo Sacer,* trans. Daniel Heller-Roazen (Stanford: Stanford University Press, 1998).

10. Giorgio Agamben, *State of Exception,* trans. Kevin Attell (Chicago: University of Chicago Press, 2005).

11. Lawrence Grossberg, *Caught in the Crossfire: Kids, Politics, and America's Future* (Boulder: Paradigm Publishers, 2005), p. 112.

12. Thomas Friedman, *The Lexus and the Olive Tree* (New York: Anchor, 2000), p. 373.

13. Cited in Mark Rupert, "The Anti-Friedman Page." Available online at http://www.maxwell.syr.edu/maxpages/faculty/merupert/Anti-Friedman.htm.

14. Grossberg, *Caught in the Crossfire,* p. 117.

15. Jim Lobe, "45 Million Children to Die in Next Decade Due to Rich Countries' Miserliness," *OneWorld.Net* (December 6, 2004). Available online at www.commondreams.org/headlines04/1206–06.htm.

16. Catherine McAloon, "UNICEF: Poverty, War, HIV Hurting Children," *Associated Press* (December 9, 2004). Available online at http://www.aegis.com/news/ads/2004/AD042515.html.

17. Jim Lobe, "45 Million Children to Die in Next Decade Due to Rich Countries' Miserliness," *OneWorld.Net* (December 6, 2004). Available online at www.commondreams.org/headlines04/1206–06.htm.

18. Carol Bellamy, "The World's Broken Promises to Our Children," *Boston Globe* (December 18, 2004). Available online at www.commondreams.org/views04/1218–01.htm.

19. Paul Krugman, "Looting the Future," *New York Times* (December 5, 2003), p. A27.

20. "Economic Recovery Failed to Benefit Much of the Population in 2004," *Center on Budget and Policy Priorities* (August 30, 2005). Available online at www.cbpp.org/8–30–05pov.htm.

21. Cesar Chelala, "Rich Man, Poor Man: Hungry Children in America," *Seattle Times* (January 4, 2006). Available online at http://www.commondreams.org/views06/0104–24.htm.

22. Gar Alperovitz, "Another World Is Possible," *Mother Jones* (January/February 2006), p. 68.

23. Ngugi Wa Thiong'O, "Europhone or African Memory: The Challenge of Pan-Africanist Intellectuals in the Era of Globalization," in *African Intellectuals: Rethinking Politics, Language, Gender and Development,* ed. Thandika Mkandawire (London: Zed Books, 2005), p. 154.

24. What now seems a typical occurrence is the takeover of school boards by right-wing Christian fundamentalists who then impose the teaching of creationism on the schools. See, for example, Associated Press, "Wisconsin School OKs Creationism Teaching," *Common Dreams News Center* (November 6, 2004); available online at http://www.commondreams.org/headlines04/1106–08.htm. The attack on science in the schools has, of course, been dealt a severe setback with the recent court ruling forbidding the teaching of intelligent design in the high school biology curriculum in Dover, Pennsylvania.

25. Cited in Grey Myre, "Israelis' Anger at Evangelist May Delay Christian Center," *New York Times* (January 12, 2006), p. A12.

26. Esther Kaplan, *With God on Their Side: How Christian Fundamentalists Trampled Science, Policy, and Democracy in George W. Bush's White House* (New York: The New Press, 2004), p. 13.

27. Grossberg, *Caught in the Crossfire,* p. 229.

28. Cited in Laura Flanders, "Bush's Hit List: Teens and Kids," *Common Dreams News Center* (February 13, 2005). Available online at www.commondreams.org/views05/0213–11.htm.

29. Frank Rich, "The Year of Living Indecently," *New York Times* (February 6, 2005), p. AR1.

30. Rich, "I Saw Jackie Mason Kissing Santa Claus," p. A8.

31. See, especially, Noah Feldman, *Divided by God* (New York: Farrar, Straus and Giroux, 2005).

32. This charge comes from a report issued by the conservative group American Council of Trustees and Alumni (ACTA), founded by Lynne Cheney (spouse of Vice President Dick Cheney) and Joseph Lieberman (Democratic senator). See Jerry L. Martin and Anne D. Neal, *Defending Civilization: How Our Universities Are Failing America and What Can Be Done About It* (February 2002). Available online at http://www.goacta.org/publications/Reports/defciv.pdf. ACTA also posted on its website a list of 115 statements made by allegedly "un-American professors."

33. See "Forum: A Chilly Climate on the Campuses," *Chronicle of Higher Education* (September 9, 2005), pp. B7–B13.

34. "The Dirty Thirty" is available online at http://www.uclaprofs.com/articles/dirtythirty.html.

35. Andrew Jones, "Open Letter from the Bruin Alumni Association." Available online at http://www.bruinalumni.com/aboutus.html.

36. Ibid.

37. Piper Fogg, "Independent Alumni Group Offers $100 Bounties to UCLA Students Who Ferret Out Classroom Bias," *Chronicle of Higher Education* (January 19, 2005). Available online at http://chronicle.com/daily/2006/01/2006011904n.htm.

38. For a much more detailed account of this type of attack on higher education, see Henry A. Giroux and Susan Searls Giroux, *Take Back Higher Education* (New York: Palgrave, 2005).

39. On the relationship between democracy and the media, see Robert W. McChesney, *Rich Media, Poor Democracy: Communication Politics in Dubious Times* (New York: The New Press, 1999); and John Nichols and Robert W. McChesney, *Tragedy: How the American Media Sell Wars, Spin Elections, and Destroy Democracy* (New York: The New Press, 2006).

40. Robert W. McChesney and John Nichols, *Our Media,*

Not Theirs: The Democratic Struggle Against Corporate Media (New York: Seven Stories, 2002), pp. 52–53.

41. Rory O'Conner, "United States of Fear," *AlterNet* (January 13, 2005). Available online at www.alternet.org/story/30801.

42. Richard J. Bernstein, *The Abuse of Evil: The Corruption of Politics and Religion Since 9/11* (London: Polity, 2005), p. 26.

43. Frank Rich, "The Wiretappers That Couldn't Shoot Straight," *New York Times* (January 8, 2006), p. WK15.

44. Editorial, "Bush's High Crimes," *The Nation* 28:2 (January 9/16, 2006), p. 3.

45. Bill O'Reilly exemplifies this type of demagoguery; see the *Think Progress* editorial "O'Reilly Resorts to McCarthyism, Plans to Publish Online Enemies List," *ThinkProgress.Org* (November 14, 2005). Available online at http://thinkprogress.org/2005/11/14/oreilly-mccarthyism/. Another typical example is Ann Coulter's tirade against liberals who question Bush's policies; see Media Matters, "Coulter on MSNBC and FOX: She Compared Bill Clinton to O.J.; Called Americans Who Don't Support Bush 'Traitors,'" *Media Matters for America* (June 25, 2004); available online at http://mediamatters.org/items/200406250002.

46. Hannah Arendt, *Men in Dark Times* (New York: Harcourt Brace, 1983), p. viii.

47. Former Treasury Secretary Paul O'Neill, who served in the Bush administration for two years, claimed on the television program *60 Minutes* that Bush and his advisers started talking about invading Iraq only ten days after the inauguration, eight months before the tragic events of September 11th. See CBS News, "Bush Sought Way to Invade Iraq," transcript, *60 Minutes* (January 11, 2004); available online at http://www.cbsnews.com/stories/2004/01/09/60minutes/main592330.shtml. For a chronicle of the lies coming out of the Bush administration, see David Corn,

The Lies of George Bush (New York: Crown, 2003). On the environment, see Seth Borenstein, "Environment Worsened Under Bush in Many Key Areas, Data Show," *Common Dreams News Center* (October 13, 2004); available online at http://www.commondreams.org/headlines04/1013-12.htm.

48. Paul Gilroy, *Postcolonial Melancholia* (New York: Columbia University Press, 2005), p. 142.

49. Samuel P. Huntington, *The Challenge to America's Identity* (New York: Simon and Schuster, 2004).

50. On Robertson's statement, see Kaplan, *With God on Their Side*, p. 13.

51. Isabel Hilton, "The 800lb Gorilla in American Foreign Policy," *The Guardian/UK* (July 28, 2004). Available online at http://www.guardian.co.uk/print/0,3858,4980261-103390,00.html.

52. Andrew J. Bacevich, *The New American Militarism* (New York: Oxford University Press, 2005), p. 1.

53. Tony Judt, "The New World Order," *New York Review of Books* (July 14, 2005), p. 16.

54. Ibid., p. 16.

55. For the Mills reference, see C. Wright Mills, *The Power Elite* (New York: Oxford University Press, 1956; reprinted in 1993), p. 222. The quotation is from Bacevich, *New American Militarism*, p. 2.

56. Bacevich, *New American Militarism*, p. 6.

57. Penn State News Release, "Penn State's Spanier to Chair National Security Board" (September 16, 2005).

58. Ibid.

59. COINTELPRO was the code name for the FBI's counterintelligence program, which operated between 1956 and 1971. The government used secret surveillance techniques, political harassment, and sometimes violence to obstruct alleged dissenters accused of being un-American. Many of these alleged terrorists targeted by the FBI were black, and two of them—Black Panther Party members

Fred Hampton and Mark Clark—were assassinated by the Chicago Police.

60. David A. Gabbard and Kenneth Saltman, eds., *Education as Enforcement* (New York: Routledge, 2003).

61. I take up the issue of zero tolerance in great detail in Henry A. Giroux, *The Terror of Neoliberalism* (Boulder: Paradigm Publishers, 2004). See also William Lyons and Julie Drew, *Punishing Schools: Fear and Citizenship in American Public Education* (Ann Arbor: University of Michigan Press, 2006).

62. See C. Schaeffer-Duffy, "Feeding the Military Machine," *National Catholic Reporter* (March 28, 2003). Available online at http://www.natcath.com/MNCR_online/archives/032803/032803a.html.

63. Michael Hardt and Antonio Negri, *Multitude: War and Democracy in the Age of Empire* (New York: Penguin Press, 2004), pp. 12–13.

64. Maureen Dowd, "The Red Zone," *New York Times* (November 4, 2004), p. A27.

65. David Theo Goldberg, "The Sovereign Smirk," *Open Democracy* (November 3, 2004), p. 3.

66. Zygmunt Bauman, *Liquid Life* (London: Polity Press, 2005), p. 14.

67. See Arif Dirlik, *Global Modernity* (Boulder: Paradigm Publishers, 2006).

68. Jacques Derrida, "No One Is Innocent: A Discussion with Jacques Derrida About Philosophy in the Face of Terror," *Sueddeutsche Zeitung* (September 21, 2001). Available online at http://www.hudsoncress.org/html/library/western-philosophy/derrida%20–%20A%20discussion%20with%20Derrida%20on%20Terror.pdf.

Index

138

FEMA. *See* Federal Emergency
  Management Agency
Financial Times, on budget
  proposal, 38
Flaherty, Jordan: on
  incarceration rate, 54
Fontenot, Anthony, 52
Ford, Henry, 94
foreign policy, 25, 85–86, 101;
  Christian evangelicals and,
  90, 94; empire-driven, 80;
  militarism and, 105
Foucault, Michel: biopolitics
  and, 12–17; biopower and,
  13, 14, 21; modernity and,
  15–16; panopticon of, 19
Fox News, 49, 50–51, 98, 99
Frank, Barney: on ethnic
  cleansing, 61
freedom, 113; democracy
  and, 73, 75, 85, 112;
  transformation of, 84
freedom movements, 31;
  radical party and, 67
free market, 22, 24, 46, 86;
  neoliberalism and, 85
free trade, 47, 84
Fregoso, Rosa Linda, 18
Friedman, Thomas, 84, 85
Friends of Bush, 59
Fukuyama, Francis, 124n102
fundamentalism, 27, 57, 70,
  80; democracy and, 76;
  economic, 114; globalization
  and, 89; militaristic,
  114. *See also* market
  fundamentalism; religious
  fundamentalism

gender extermination, politics
  of, 18
Gigot, Paul, 32
globalization, 68, 113;
  fundamentalism and, 89;
  social consequences of, 23
global south, threat from, 103

global warming, 88, 89, 93
Goldberg, David Theo, 104;
  on Bush reelection, 109;
  on disposability/recovery,
  61–62; on privatization, 36
Goldwater, Barry, 2
governance, 26, 58, 75; failure
  of, 39, 87
government: attack on, 32, 33,
  41; social services and, 37
Graham, Billy, 91
Graham, Franklin, 91
Great Society, 45, 86
Greider, William, 27–28,
  121n71
Grossberg, Lawrence: on free
  market/neoliberalism, 85
Group of Eight (G-8), 89
Gulf Coast: recovery on,
  58–60; as war zone, 56–57
Gulf War: censorship of, 4–5;
  media coverage of, 3, 5

Halliburton, 58, 59
Hampton, Fred, 137n59
Hannity, Sean, 102
Hardt, Michael, 20, 108;
  biopolitics and, 12, 15, 16–
  17; biopower and, 14–15;
  modernity and, 15–16
Harvey, David: on
  accumulation/
  dispossession, 82
Hastert, Dennis: on New
  Orleans rebuilding, 58
health care, 29, 67; access
  to, 85; crisis in, 34, 90;
  vouchers for, 59
health insurance, 10; lack of,
  34, 35, 36, 87, 88
Hersh, Seymour M., 6, 79
higher education, 71, 77, 108;
  attack on, 72, 95, 96, 97,
  134n38; military-industrial
  complex and, 106; national
  security state and, 106

◊

About the Author

Henry A. Giroux is the Global Television Network Chair and Professor in the English and Cultural Studies Department at McMaster University in Canada. His most recent books include: *Border Crossings* (Routledge 2005); *Schooling and the Struggle for Public Life* (Paradigm 2005); *Take Back Higher Education: Race, Youth, and the Crisis of Democracy in the Post Civil Rights Era* (Palgrave Macmillan 2004); *The Terror of Neoliberalism* (Paradigm 2004); and *The Abandoned Generation: Democracy Beyond the Culture of Fear* (Palgrave 2003), co-authored with Susan Searls Giroux. His primary research areas are cultural studies, youth studies, critical pedagogy, popular culture, media studies, social theory, and the politics of higher and public education.